ISBN 978-1-333-23401-0
PIBN 10477012

English
Français
Deutsche
Italiano
Español
Português

www.forgottenbooks.com

Mythology Photography **Fiction**
Fishing Christianity **Art** Cooking
Essays Buddhism Freemasonry
Medicine **Biology** Music **Ancient**
Egypt Evolution Carpentry Physics
Dance Geology **Mathematics** Fitness
Shakespeare **Folklore** Yoga Marketing
Confidence Immortality Biographies
Poetry **Psychology** Witchcraft
Electronics Chemistry History **Law**
Accounting **Philosophy** Anthropology
Alchemy Drama Quantum Mechanics
Atheism Sexual Health **Ancient History**
Entrepreneurship Languages Sport
Paleontology Needlework Islam
Metaphysics Investment Archaeology
Parenting Statistics Criminology
Motivational

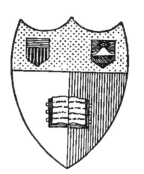

The date shows when this volume was taken.

To renew this book copy the call No. and give
to the librarian.

HOME USE RULES

All Books subject to recall

All borrowers must register in the library to borrow books for home use.

All books must be returned at end of college year for inspection and repairs.

Limited books must be returned within the four week limit and not renewed.

Students must return all books before leaving town Officers should arrange for the return of books wanted during their absence from town

Volumes of periodicals and of pamphlets are held in the library as much as possible. For special purposes they are given out for a limited time.

Borrowers should not use their library privileges for the benefit of other persons

Books of special value and gift books, when the giver wishes it, are not allowed to circulate.

Readers are asked to report all cases of books marked or mutilated.

Do not deface books by marks and writing.

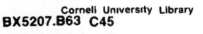

THE LIFE AND TIMES OF
MARTIN BLAKE B.D.

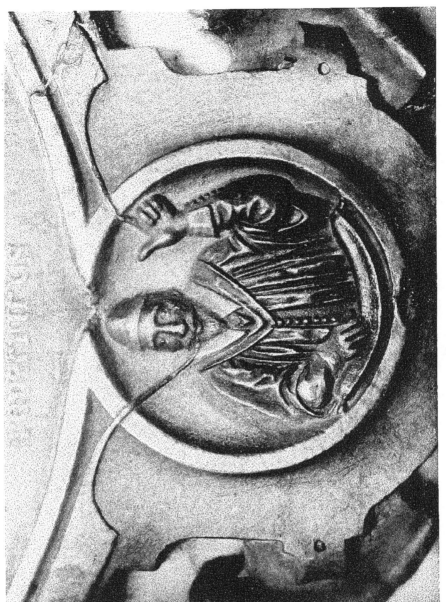

MARTIN BLAKE
From the Blake Monument

THE LIFE AND TIMES OF MARTIN BLAKE B.D.

(1593-1673) VICAR OF BARNSTAPLE AND PREBENDARY OF EXETER CATHEDRAL WITH SOME ACCOUNT OF HIS CONFLICTS WITH THE PURITAN LECTURERS AND PERSECUTIONS ও ও ও BY JOHN FREDERICK CHANTER M.A. RECTOR OF PARRACOMBE DEVON ও ও ও ও ও

LONDON: JOHN LANE, THE BODLEY HEAD
NEW YORK: JOHN LANE COMPANY MCMX

Turnbull & Spears, Printers, Edinburgh

PREFACE

THE story of Martin Blake and his persecutions had always been a subject of great interest to me. And when chance and the kindness of my friend Oswyn Murray, Esq., threw in my way a mass of original letters and documents connected with Blake, I determined to write a short life of him for our County Literary and Archæological Association.

Finding it, however, impossible to condense the materials to a length suitable for such a publication, yet thinking it desirable to preserve for posterity these fast-decaying records, I have supplemented them with facts gathered from many sources, and cast them into a form in which I trust they may be of some interest, not only to Devonshire men, but perhaps also to a wider public.

J. FREDERICK CHANTER.

PARRACOMBE RECTORY,
June 1909.

AUTHORITIES

MS. Autobiography of Martin Blake.
Original MS. Letters.
Walker MSS., Bodleian Library.
Tanner MSS., Bodleian Library.
Additional MSS., British Museum.
Lansdowne MSS., British Museum.
Corporation Records, Barnstaple and Plymouth.
Parochial Registers and Records, Barnstaple, Plymouth,
    and King's Nympton.
Sufferings of the Clergy. Walker (Church in the West
    Edition, with Hingeston Randolph's notes).
Calamy Abridgment of Baxter's History and continuations.
History of the English Church, 1640-1660. Shaw.
Registers of Exeter College, Oxford. Boase.
State Papers. Domestic series, P.R.O.
Composition Books, P.R.O.
Journal, House of Commons.
MS. Episcopal Registers, Diocese of Exeter.
Worthies of Devon. Prince.
Contemporary Pamphlets, British Museum.
Barnstaple during the Civil War. Cotton.
Lambeth MSS.

CONTENTS

CHAPTER I

EARLY LIFE, EDUCATION, AND RELIGIOUS POSITION

1593-1626

CHAPTER II

THE VICAR OF BARNSTAPLE AND THE LECTURERS

1626-1640

The Life of Martin Blake B.D.

Letters of Bishop Hall and Hanmer—Blake accused of Arminianism—Quarrel with Crompton—Recorder appointed arbitrator—Crompton leaves—The Canons of 1640—Blake's letter to Hakewill . . . . . .

CHAPTER III

THE VICAR AND THE CIVIL WAR

1640-1646

George Peard—Thomas Matthews—Ship money—Blake refuses to pay his assessment—Convented before his Bishop—His remonstrance—Council of War—Vicar takes no part in politics—Desire for peace—Declaration of Justices of the Peace for the county—Suppressed by Peard—Blake gets a copy of it—Conference of townsmen desiring peace—Blake draws up considerations for a peace—Sends it to the Council for War—Considerations ordered to be burnt at the High Cross—Deputation to Prince Maurice—Mayor, aldermen, and vicar's letter to the Prince—Surrender of Barnstaple—Mayor's letter to Colonel Digby—Blake's letter to Philip Francis, Mayor of Plymouth—Blake's disappointment at renewal of war—Death of Blake's wife and father—Keeps aloof during Royalist occupation—Final surrender of Barnstaple . . . .

CHAPTER IV

BLAKE'S FIRST PERSECUTION AND ITS END

1646-1648

The Committee for Plundered Ministers—The nine-handed petition against Blake—The vicar summoned before the County Committee—The town petitions in his favour—Appears before the Committee—Vicar suspended—Clerk alters sentence to sequestration—Blake's farewell letter to his parishioners—The plague at Barnstaple—No one to bury the dead—Letter to Sir John Bampfield—Tooker's second petition to Committee for Plundered Ministers—Blake sequestrated—Blake appeals to the Committee—Blake discharged—Tooker and Peard's fresh petition—Plundered Ministers Committee order case to be argued—Documents

Contents

CHAPTER V

RETURN TO BARNSTAPLE AND THE SECOND PERSECUTION

1648-1659

CHAPTER VI

THE VICAR'S LAST YEARS AND DEATH

1660-1673

ILLUSTRATIONS

xiii

THE LIFE AND TIMES OF
MARTIN BLAKE B.D.

: : THE LIFE OF : :
MARTIN BLAKE B.D.

CHAPTER I

EARLY LIFE, EDUCATION, AND RELIGIOUS POSITION

1593-1626

Foreword—The Blakes of Plymouth—Birth—
Education at Plymouth old Grammar School—
Choice of a Profession—His father's opposition—
Runs away from home—Goes to Oxford—At
Balliol College—Removes to Exeter College—His
tutors and life at Oxford—Takes his Degree—
Remains at Oxford as a Divinity Student—Called
back to Plymouth—Hasty ordination—Meets his
future wife—Death of his mother—Her character
—Marriage—Mrs Blake's relatives—Rev. John
Downe—Dr George Hakewill—Blake's religious
views—Presented to Kings Nympton—Ordained
Priest—Frequent visits to Barnstaple—Takes his
B.D. Degree.

THE life of a Devonshire country-town
parson, whose lot was cast in the stormy
period of the seventeenth century, may seem to
present little of new interest : for the story of

A   I

The Life of Martin Blake B.D.

many a divine of that time who played a prominent part on one side or the other in the great conflict between Catholicism and Puritanism which raged during the whole of that century, has already been written,—but mostly by strong partisans of one view or the other, who saw only the rights of their own side.

But it is not my purpose to enter into either theological or civil disputes ; and the life of Martin Blake, while perhaps specially interesting to Devonshire men, as a link that binds together the two principal maritime towns of North and South Devon (Barnstaple and Plymouth), has a wider interest as typical of that of one of the moderate Churchmen of the time of whom it would be difficult to say to which party they belonged : for in different points they were in sympathy sometimes with one party, and sometimes with the other. Indeed, very little has been written from the standpoint of that very large number of clergy who, during the different crises of the long period of the English Reformation (1530-1660), sought to reconcile their consciences and convictions with the various changes imposed on them by those who for the time being were in authority ;—Vicars of Bray, some have styled them, but the truth is that they were determined to cling and remain steadfast to their branch of the Church, even in her deepest

The Life of Martin Blake B.D.

troubles, trusting that the storms which distressed her and them would soon pass over.

Dr Walker, in his well-known book, entitled "The Sufferings of the Clergy,' has given a long account of Blake's sufferings and persecutions during the great rebellion, but gives, I think, a very false impression of Blake's views and opinions : for from Walker's details we should be inclined to class Blake with those of the loyalist clergy who were more politicians than priests, while his real life, as shown in his own words and letters, suggest more of that fervent personal piety that it has been the fashion to associate more particularly with the better sort of those whom we call Puritans, rather than with the Cavalier clergy, though this spirit is to be found by the impartial seeker in the finer characters on both sides. Walker, indeed, gives only a one-sided view of Blake's life, and for only a few years of it, and that not altogether a true one ; he represents the Rev. Jonathan Hanmer as a factious lecturer thrust upon Blake, with whom he had to bear, lest they should get him a second time dispossessed (Walker, pt. ii., p. 196), whereas the two men were friends and connections, Hanmer being Mrs Blake's first cousin.

The late R. W. Cotton, in his exhaustive work

The Life of Martin Blake B.D.

on Barnstaple and Devon, during the civil-war period, totally ignored the part played by Martin Blake in the varied fortunes of the town during that period. In the last chapter of his book he says : " Throughout the whole of the period over which this relation has extended, his [*i.e.* Blake's] name has not occurred, and it might be inferred he took no active part whatever in local politics," and, after giving a brief abstract of Walker's account, ends by saying : " So much, and perhaps too much, of Martin Blake" (Cotton's "Civil War," pp. 527-530). But Cotton, who was so careful in his local detail, was writing from imperfect data ; in his account of the negotiations that led up to the surrender of Barnstaple to Prince Maurice on September 2, 1643, he says : " It was evidently the result of previous conferences ; " but of these conferences, the events that led up to it, and Blake's efforts for peace, Cotton had no knowledge, or he would have modified his views. In this story of Blake's life I have relied entirely on contemporary documents and letters, and for the early part of this life on an hitherto unknown MS., partly in ordinary writing and partly in a curious shorthand, being part of an unfinished autobiography of Martin Blake in his own handwriting, entitled :

" A humble reflection upon the various passages of the providence of God toward my poore

The Life of Martin Blake B.D.

unworthy self through the whole course of my life hitherto.   Ann° D^{ni} 1660."

This MS. was sent by Blake's granddaughter Joan, through Mrs Browning, widow of the Rev. George Browning, Vicar of Barnstaple, to Dr Walker, to use in his account of Blake, and is endorsed in Walker's handwriting :

"A MS. of part of the life of the excellent Mr Blake of Barnstaple, wch I had by me, but by forgetfulness I omitted to incorporate with ye account of him in my book.

"J. W.

"*May* 1714."

It was my intention to have given this document in full, but the difficulties of the shorthand portions prevented my doing so, though I have quoted freely from it ; but the style of it may be judged from the opening passage, which is as follows :—

"It pleased Alm: God who hath made of one blood all nations of men for to dwell on the face of the earth and hath determ^d the times before appointed and the bounds of their Hab^{con} to give unto me an entraunce into this world at Plym a famous seaport in ye County of Devon.   I was born there on Thursday 7^{br} 20 anno 1593° and yere also Bap^{td} the next L^{ds} day after, being ye 23° of ye same mo.   Nicholas Blake a native of the

The Life of Martin Blake B.D.

same Town, & by calling a M^{cht} was my father and his wife Joan descended of the ffamily of the Goddards born at Kingsbridge (a Town about 13 miles distant from Plym.) was my mother; they were both of them (at that time) young beginners, but very industryous in their way having their hearts well seasoned with ye love & ffear of God & (for wch I am ever very deeply bound to magnifie the divine goodnes) very carefull and consciencious in the training up of their children. As in other respects so especially in the way of true religion, very frequent they were (both of them) in their Holy Counsels wch also they seconded all along with their own vertuous Ex^{ples} and (as a meanes to make the whole yet more effectuall) they were not wanting in their prayers to God for his Blessing, as upon us so upon their endeavours on our behalf: so that wherein any of us came short of what we should bee must be imputed rather to our own neglect than their want of care."

Blake's style of writing may be judged from this extract—though it is perhaps less prolix and involved than his sermons and other writings.

The Blakes of Plymouth appear to have been a somewhat obscure family there; they do not seem to have been in any way connected with the family of Blake of Comb, in the county of Devon,

The Life of Martin Blake B.D.

of which a pedigree is given by Vivian in his "Visitation of Cornwall," nor with John Blake, Rector of Charles, North Devon, 1568-1614, many of whose descendants held livings in Devon; neither can I find any connection with the better-known Somerset family of the same name, though the famous Admiral Blake interceded for Martin Blake during his persecutions. Martin Blake says his family were old residents and natives of Plymouth, but the first of them I find is William Blake, probably grandfather of Martin, whose name appears in a deed, dated July 14, 1561, in the records of the Corporation of Plymouth, as one of the founders of the old Grammar School. His father, Nicholas Blake, was born in 1552, and, by reason of his father's early death, was brought up by his mother, who is described as a very grave and serious matron, who educated her son in the severest way that was at that time in use. Nicholas Blake married first Joan Goddard, on November 29, 1590, at St Andrew's Church, Plymouth, and by her had a family of seven sons and seven daughters, most of whom died young (Mrs Blake died in 1619—" Buried Dec. 17, 1619, Joan, wyfe of Mr Nic⁵ Blake.—Reg. St Andrew, Plymouth"); and, secondly, Jane, some connection of Matthew Sutcliffe, Dean of Exeter; his widow, Anne Sutcliffe, calls her my cousin. By the second wife there were two sons and three daughters.

The Life of Martin Blake B.D.

Nicholas Blake of Plymouth was, as his son tells us, a merchant, and prospered, and became mayor of his native town in 1625, which honour, however, was his undoing, as during his year of office he advanced large sums of money to the Government, in connection with the Cadiz expedition, and was unable to obtain repayment from a Government who were always short of money. He had to sell his estates, and was imprisoned for debt. After his release he left Plymouth, and joined his son Martin at Barnstaple, and died there in 1645-6 and was buried near the South Wall of the Parish Church (wills of Nicholas Blake, prov^d, April 9, 1646, and Martin Blake, dated September 1656). His second wife, Jane Blake, was also buried there, July 16, 1674, at a very advanced age.

Martin Blake was the second son of the first marriage, and was born September 20, 1593, and baptized September 23, 1593, at St Andrew's, Plymouth. Like his father, he was very strictly brought up. In his childhood, he tells us, he was "too much pronnes to waggishness and vanity," and his father "carried over him a stricter hand of discipline, which, though it seemed then to his childish fancy very harsh, was yet alternately so intermingled with expressions of tender love, and all along so sweetened with the discrete indulgence of his mother, that, as they aimed it, so indeed he found it himself, as it were, set in equall

8

The Life of Martin Blake B.D.

balance betwixt awe and encouragement." This description of the home influence and discipline in the merchant's house at Plymouth, which I have taken from Martin Blake's own words, gives us a clear insight into his youthful surroundings —the strict, stern father, and the affectionate, indulgent mother.

At an early age Martin was sent with his elder brother William to the old Grammar School at Plymouth, his first master being William Kempe, an M.A. of Cambridge, and both an author and a poet. This school had been founded in 1561 by the Corporation at Plymouth, and was carried on in the old chapel of the almshouse or hospital that had been licensed by Bishop Lacy in 1450, and had passed from the Priory of Plymton with other manorial property to the Mayor and Corporation. Kempe soon gave way to a Mr Moore, whom Bishop Cotton describes as an excellent good scholar, and who had made as many good scholars as any man in the county. Moore left in 1605 for a living, and was succeeded by the Rev. John Worth, a master whom Blake ever looked back on with affectionate remembrance, both for his teaching and for counsels given him in private in the master's study, the old chamber over the almshouse chapel.

Both of the brothers remained at this school till early in 1608, when their father, desirous of settling his sons in such professions as should best suit their dispositions and abilities, called them one evening into a room apart and said : " My sons, it is now time for me to determine of setting you in some good way for the future comfortable passage of your lives, and because I would gladly suit your callings to your inclinations, let me hear from you which way your desires are most bent, whether to be bred up as scholars or otherwise to apply yourselves to some other course."

Both William and Martin replied that they were willing to submit to his more able judgment and election.

The father being somewhat instant to feel which way their genius did lean, insisted still on his former demand : " On what calling are your desires set ? "

William answered first : " I most incline to the calling of a merchant such as is my honoured father." And then Martin replied : " Sir, at present I desire continuance at the school, in order that I may make some further progress in learning."

His father immediately replied : " My son, what is the reason of your choice ?—do you vainly conceive that that kind of life is more full of ease, and so more pleasing to a slothful disposition ?— be advised that if you so think, you will deceive yourself, because that course of life, if rightly

The Life of Martin Blake B.D.

followed, is of all others the most difficult and laborious, and such as will require more diligence in the pursuit than peradventure you are yet aware of. Tell me, therefore, and tell me truly, what is it in particular which you do specially aim at in this choice?"

Martin was somewhat daunted at this reiteration of his father's demand, but being still urged by him to freely speak what he had in his thoughts, after a pause, replied "That if his father so liked and God would be pleased to fit him for it, his desire was to serve God in the work of the ministry." Nicholas Blake made no reply to this request, but after remaining silent for a while dismissed both his sons with some wholesome counsels for their present life.

Soon after this interview William Blake, the elder son, was sent abroad to one of his father's foreign correspondents to learn the details of a merchant's work and foreign languages, and Martin went back to his school.

Within a year after this, Nicholas Blake, to make a further trial of his son, removed Martin from school, and told him he was making arrangements to send him to France that he might learn the language. This cast him into a great sadness: on one hand not wishing to disobey his father, and on the other hand, dreading to give up the hope of serving in the ministry of the Church, to

The Life of Martin Blake B.D.

which he was persuaded God had called him; so he determined to lay the matter first before his mother, who had always been so tender and indulgent to him, then before his grandmother, who had so often instilled into him the need of obeying God's voice, and also before the Rev. Henry Wallis, his parish priest, and especially before his schoolmaster and friend, the Rev. John Worth, asking them all to intercede with his father to allow him to continue his studies to fit himself for the ministerial calling, and in due time to send him to the University.

They all did as he desired, and Martin once more resumed his studies, but his father, by often speaking of removing him again, kept him on the tenter hooks, fearful, as he often told him after, that he had not laid his desires on the right foundation. So things went on till Martin had entered his seventeenth year, when he could bear the suspense no longer, and, thinking that by no other way could he induce his father to believe in the reality of his desires, he determined to secretly leave Plymouth and his home, and make his way on foot to Oxford, where he thought he might enter himself as a poor scholar. He carried out his purpose, and was some miles on the way ere his parents noted his absence. They enquired in every direction for him, but all in vain. No trace could be found of him for two days, till a traveller arrived at Plymouth, who reported having passed him walking towards Exeter. His father immediately took horse, rode after him, and overtook him just as he arrived at Exeter, and brought him back with him to Plymouth, where his mother received her lost son with such demonstrations of love, affection, and tears that he was touched to the quick, and asked his parents' forgiveness for his foolish prank, laying before them the reasons that had impelled him to it.

Nicholas Blake was, however, convinced that his son was firmly set on taking Holy Orders, and in December 1610 set out for London, taking Martin with him. On arriving there he sought counsel from his London correspondent as to the best college at Oxford to send his son to, and was recommended by him to enter him at Balliol. This advice he accepted, and returning home *via* Oxford, settled Martin there under the tutorship of John Abbot, who had been recommended to him as a grave, learned, and good tutor.

Martin Blake, however, remained but a few months at Balliol. His father, on returning to Plymouth, was counselled by many of his friends to remove his son to Exeter College, as being especially the west country college, and accordingly Martin was removed to it, and on June 7,

The Life of Martin Blake B.D.

1611, matriculated as of Exeter College, his first tutor there being Mr William Batteshill, a young man who had not yet taken his M.A. degree, but had recently been chosen a Fellow of the College, and was reputed to be dexterous for bringing on young students in the first part of academical learning. Here the next eight years of Martin Blake's life was mainly spent, and Exeter College imprinted on his character and belief an impress that was never entirely obliterated. The Rector of Exeter, Dr John Prideaux, was the leading theologian and champion of the anti-Laudian school, and under his government Exeter was characterised by a curious blend of Royalism and Puritanism. Prideaux's reputation drew members to the college, not only from the west of England, with which it had an old traditional connection, but from all over England, and even from the Continent. Anthony Wood mentions Germans, Danes, Hollanders, and Swiss as attracted there. But Prideaux, though a Puritan, was never an extreme man, he belonged to the church wing of the party, and was strongly opposed to the non-conforming section, and so might be more properly described as holding a middle position in religion, and was asked by Laud afterwards to revise Chillingworth's famous book, "The Religion of Protestants." His lectures on theology (which coloured much of

The Life of Martin Blake B.D.

Blake's views in after life) were much admired, and he is described as "Oxonii gloria, ecclesiæ lumen maximus, veritatis Anglicanæ propugnator summus."

Among Blake's contemporaries who were at Exeter were the Hydes, Sir Richard Spottiswoode, Sir Bevil Grenville, Sir John Arundell, Digory Polwhele, the Duke of Hamilton; such well-known Devonshire names as Carys and Champernownes; and also such well-known parliamentarians as John Eliot, William Strode, John Maynard, and William Noye.

Martin Blake, however, cannot be said to have been intimate with any of these. The little circle of his particular friends were all more or less unimportant personages and divinity students. They were: John Bury and Thomas Stafford, both Devonshire men, Robert Petifare, from Gloucestershire, Anthony Standard, Thomas Browne, and William Roweston. Anthony Standard after became a Fellow of Exeter. Browne and Bury, after Blake's departure from Oxford, were both incorporated at Cambridge. Blake and Petifare became country parsons.

The divinity lectures chiefly attended by them were those of a Devonshire and Exeter man, Lawrence Bodley, a nephew of the great Sir Thomas Bodley, afterwards Rector of Clyst Hidon, Devon, and Canon of Exeter. Dr

The Life of Martin Blake B.D.

Hakewill says of him in a letter to Archbishop Usher: "Of his sobriety, gravity, piety, and every-way sufficiency, I have had a long trial, and were he not so near me in blood, I could easily afford him a larger testimony ("Life of Usher," 1686, p. 398). Martin Blake took his Bachelor's degree on May 24, 1614, after which he still remained at Oxford, pursuing his theological studies at the Bodleian, where he read through a course of all the early fathers and the great writers of the early Reformation period, as well as attending the lectures of the divinity professors.

During the whole of his stay at Oxford, his correspondence with his parents was very regular, and his father's letters to him are full of counsel and advice, which Martin says preserved him from sundry extravagances which otherwise in all likelihood he would have run into, and all the while his mother (like another Monica) never ceased to write and strive with him. On Feb. 25, 1616, he proceeded to his Master's degree, but shortly after this he heard from his father news of the death of his elder brother, William, and soon there was another letter from his father requesting him to make haste down to Plymouth and stay with his father and mother in their great trouble. Blake immediately set out for his old home and remained there some six months, when, seeing his parents much recovered, he expressed to them his desire to return to Oxford and resume his studies. His father, however, desired that as now Martin was the eldest son, that he should enter his father's business, and spoke of disinheriting him and leaving all his lands to one of his younger sons if Martin was unwilling to assist him. Martin, he said, had been a great expense to him at Oxford, and if he was unwilling to take up the elder son's burden he must not expect the elder son's portion. In perplexity, Martin had long discourses and talks with his mother; he told her that if he must needs be deprived of outward and worldly advantages, his desire was to have his father and mother's free consent to go on in his design for the service of God in the ministry, it being the thing to which from his youth he had devoted himself and aimed his studies.

His mother assured him that she entirely approved of his desires, and did not believe his father would cross them, and then praying with great earnestness to God to bless her son, she said she would talk to his father and do her best for him. Shortly after this he returned to Oxford with the consent of both his parents, but in less than six months he received another urgent summons to return home. On receiving the letter Blake felt the matter must be settled at

The Life of Martin Blake B.D.

once, and he went to the Bishop of Oxford, John Howson, formerly student and fellow of Christchurch, who had lately been consecrated to that see (September 12, 1618), to request him to admit him, after due examination, to Holy Orders. He was at once accepted by the bishop, and at the next ordination Blake was ordained Deacon, as he says, to his own great content and satisfaction. Almost immediately after he received an express order from his father to come to him at once, on which he went down to Plymouth, and, as he says, "did acquaint my father with what I had so lately done, hoping that he would approve thereof, which indeed he did in a more ample way than I first expected, especially after I had once appeared in publique by the earnest entreaty of a reverent minister living neere the town"; and soon the young deacon was "not difficult but easily drawn on to preach in severall congregations thereabout, and received much encouragement from many very grave and Godly divines, and especially from that worthy man and faithfull servant of Christ, Mr Samuel Mayne of Holsworthy, of nearest consanguinity with my father, and at that time a bright star in the firmament of our Church, and of great and gratious influence in those western parts, by whom I was not a little strengthened in the course I had begun."

The Life of Martin Blake B.D.

This relative was Samuel Mayne, Rector of Holsworthy (of the Plymouth family of Mayne or Meanes) of Peterhouse, Cambridge, B.A. 1586, M.A. 1590, B.D. 1598, and incorporated at Oxford, July 16, 1601 ; he became Rector of Holsworthy in 1603 ; married Hannah Gale, sister of Theophilus Gale, Rector of Kingsteignton, and Josias Gale, Rector of West Buckland, and cousin of Lawrence Bodly, Canon of Exeter; he died in 1632.

Blake's admission to Holy Orders, though he thought it would be a surprise to his father, had evidently been expected. Indeed, Mr Nicholas Blake, who was now a prosperous and rising man at Plymouth, had already anticipated it, for he had taken steps to procure him a living when he should be qualified, having purchased the next presentations of Fremington and King's Nympton. His mother had also been on the look-out for a fitting wife for him, believing that he who getteth a good wife getteth a treasure from the Lord.

The visit to his relative, Rev. Samuel Mayne, Rector of Holsworthy, which he had been encouraged to make, ostensibly for advice in his clerical career, was really for the purpose that he might meet and make the acquaintance of a young lady who was on a visit there to her relatives, Miss Elizabeth Delbridge, younger

The Life of Martin Blake B.D.

daughter of Mr John Delbridge of Barnstaple, merchant, whom Mrs Blake had aimed at as a suitable and good match for her son. The acquaintance was made with mutual satisfaction, and affairs were rapidly progressing in the direction his mother desired, when a heavy blow fell on Martin—"the sweet was mingled with ye bitterness of sorrow by the decease of my dear mother." After a very short illness, Mrs Blake died, and was buried at St Andrew's, Plymouth, December 17, 1619.

Martin had been devotedly attached to his mother: her sweetness of disposition and tender affection had attracted all his love, contrasted as it was with the apparent sternness and strictness of his father and grandmother. He speaks of her tender care and love for him in his childhood, and describes her as "a woman fairly beautiful, with those virtues that become her sex whether we look upon her as a wife, as a mother, as a guide in the ffamily, as a neighbour, as a friend, or as (in all these) a conscientious Christian, in so much that the preacher said truly at her funeral she was second to none and left behind her but few equalls in the place."

Her last words on her death-bed were to express an earnest desire that Martin would wed Elizabeth Delbridge, and so, as he says, he "alleviated his sorrow" and carried out his

The Life of Martin Blake B.D.

mother's last wish by "a marriage with that prudent and gracious young woman, Elizabeth, daughter of Mr John Delbridge, the same woman who my mother had so importunately aymed at."

By this marriage, which took place at the Church of St Peter, Barnstaple, February 28, 1619-20, a new sphere, and one that the rest of his life was mainly lived in, was opened up to Martin Blake: for he was brought into intimate connection with the Delbridge and Downe families, by whose fortunes and views his after-life was mainly moulded; so a word on these families and their connections is perhaps necessary.

They were two of the leading merchant families at Barnstaple, the Downes, who prided themselves on their ancient descent from the Downes of East Downe, were for many generations the leading men in Barnstaple and neighbourhood. Two of them had married, in a former generation, sisters of the famous Bishop Jewell, John Downe of Holsworthy marrying Joan Jewell, and Henry Downe of Barnstaple Cecily Jewell, and the family were strong upholders of the Church, and particularly that view of her "as held by the ancient fathers and general councils" which Bishop Jewell had appealed to. They must not be confounded with another Downe family, with whom also Blake was afterwards brought into contact, and who were his greatest opponents and accusers in his persecutions.

This second Downe family were extreme Puritans, and the descendants of Thomas Downe, Vicar of Stratton (1606), and Buckland Brewer (1611), by his marriage with Susanna, daughter of Nicholas Payne of Stratton. His sons were: (1) Thomas Downe, Rector of Goodleigh (1633-55), and afterwards Minister of St Edmund on the Bridge, Exeter (presented by Exeter Corporation, August 11, 1657); (2) Anthony Downe, Vicar of Northam, 1640; (3) Mark Downe, Minister of St Petrock's, Exeter (1657), and City Chaplain (September 2, 1642);— (4) Katherine Downe married to William Clyde, the intruding Rector of Instow, all four of these clerics were among the ejected ministers in 1662.

John Delbridge, father of Martin Blake's wife, was the son of Richard Delbridge of Barnstaple, baptized July 9, 1564, was thrice Mayor of Barnstaple, and Member of Parliament for the town in five parliaments. He had married, January 10, 1584, at Bishop's Tawton, Agnes, eldest daughter of Henry Downe of Barnstaple, by Cecily Jewell (married September 12, 1564, Eastdowne). By this marriage there were four children :—

(1) John Delbridge, baptized January 21,

The Life of Martin Blake B.D.

1585-6 (Barnstaple); married Martha, daughter of John Wright, Esq.; buried May 2, 1622.

(2) Mary Delbridge, baptized December 15, 1588 (Pilton); married first John Ayer, merchant, May 23, 1608 (Barnstaple), by whom she had a daughter, Martha, who married in 1630, Thomas Matthew of London, merchant, who afterwards settled at Barnstaple, and was one of the leading loyalists there in the civil war, and was twice Mayor. Secondly, Mary Delbridge married, in 1615, Rev. George Hakewill, D.D., Archdeacon of Surrey (1616), Rector of Heanton (1611-49), and Rector of Exeter College, Oxford (1642), by whom she had two sons, John and George Hakewill.

(3) Elizabeth Delbridge, baptized December 30, 1597, who married Martin Blake, as above.

(4) Richard Delbridge, who married first, Elizabeth, daughter of John Chichester, Esq., of Hall, who died December 16, 1620, and second, in 1631, Elizabeth, daughter of Humphrey Specott of Specott, Esq.

John Delbridge was for many years one of the most trusted and leading men in Barnstaple. He died at his house at Rumsum in June 1639, his wife, Agnes, having predeceased him less than a month previously. In his will he mentions his loving sons-in-law, George Hakewill, D.D.,

The Life of Martin Blake B.D.

Hakewill of Exeter, by Thomasin, daughter of John **Peryam**, was a churchman of brilliant abilities and of a moderate high type. Boswell says of him he was one of the giants by study of whom Johnson formed his style. Milton also based one of his Latin poems on Hakewill's "Apology or Declaration of the Power and Providence of God." At Oxford he had been so noted a disputant and orator, that he had been unanimously elected a Fellow of Exeter College at two years' standing. He also studied at Heidelberg, and became chaplain to Prince Charles and Archdeacon of Surrey, but shipwrecked all chance of higher promotion by writing a pamphlet against the proposed Spanish marriage, which cost him not only his chaplaincy, but also caused him to be cast into prison. On his release he retired to the country living of Heanton, though he was afterwards elected Rector of Exeter College, to which he was a great benefactor. John Downe was a fervent Churchman of a somewhat low type, like the majority of the Emmanuel-bred men ; yet we find that before his death he sent for a neighbouring clergyman to receive his confession and give him priestly absolution, and one of his published sermons is on the subject of the Blessed Virgin, being indeed the Deipara, or Mother of God.

Blake, on the other hand, had been reared in a

rather extreme Puritan school. At Oxford he was a decided Calvinist, and his mother's and grandmother's views left an impression on him that was never entirely obliterated; but his intimate relations with Hakewill and Downe considerably affected his views, as he says: "I must and doe, with all humble and hearty praise to God, acknowledge the manifold blessings which He was pleased to vouchsafe unto me by the many holy conferences, prudent counsell, and exemplarie conversations of these two eminent and gracious Divines."

Blake's position was one that was little understood in those days. He cannot be labelled either Catholic or Puritan. These two schools of thought, from the days of Elizabeth, had been ever striving against each other from within the fold of the English Church; and purposely her formulas had been so expressed as to give each a footing; both parties professed attachment and allegiance to her, and each party claimed that they were her true exponents and expressed her true spirit; and as in turn one or the other got the upper-hand, they attempted to shackle if they could not altogether suppress the other. Toleration for each other, which had been the aim of the Elizabeth statesmen, was altogether foreign to the spirit of the times, and, though heard occasionally, was but a feeble voice crying in the wilderness, and, as

The Life of Martin Blake B.D.

we find nowadays, those who profess it when a minority do not practice it when a majority.

Nowadays we should class Blake as a moderate Churchman with evangelical leanings. His early education was, as I said, decidedly low if not Puritan ; but his conferences with Dr Hakewill and Downe, whose advice he sought in his difficulties, largely modified the effects of his bringing up ; and this feeling was increased by the narrowness, bigotry, and violence of his Puritanically-inclined clerical neighbours, such as the two Downes at Goodleigh and Northam, John Hawkins at Filleigh, and the lecturers Benjamin Cox at Barnstaple and William Bartlett at Bideford. Yet even as late as 1640, we find that Blake had scruples about subscribing to the Canons of that date, and especially to the 6th, the famous "Et cetera" oath (Tanner, MS., lv., 199, Bodleian) ; but we can trace a steady movement in his views as the intolerance of the ultra Puritan party alienated him more and more from his earlier sympathies, though Blake himself was scarcely conscious of the shifting of his doctrinal standard. This comes out clearly in one of his later pulpit controversies, in the recoil from the narrow predestinarian views then so commonly held. He had preached what was practically Arminian doctrine, yet when accused of it he recoiled from any such an idea : for from his early training he had looked on Arminianism as an heresy; and so, when accused of preaching Arminianism, he exclaimed : "I can't be patient on the suspicion of Heresy." Yet he was undoubtedly progressing on the path which since not only evangelical Churchmen but even the Wesleyan Methodists have followed.

And in the story of his persecutions, which I shall tell in a later chapter, one fact stands out clear : That whatever opposition there was to his religious views, it came, not from the Puritan party, who leaned to a moderate Presbyterianism, but from those who were supporters of the militant party, commonly known as the Independants. And during the Protectorate the Puritans hated the Independants worse than the Church. Their agreement only lasted as long as the Church was a common enemy ; and as soon as the Church seemed defeated, the bitter differences between them quickly came to the surface. Throughout the whole of his ministerial career, Blake was an acceptable person to the moderate Puritans, and that element on the Corporation of Barnstaple were his consistent supporters. It was those who, to use Blake's expression, "were infected with sour leaven of Brownism," who were his inveterate opponents and persecutors when political circumstances gave them the chance.

The Life of Martin Blake B.D.

Blake for a short time after his marriage paid visits to his wife's relatives, but resided principally with his father-in-law at Rumsum, in the parish of Bishop's Tawton, and assisted occassionally at Barnstaple Parish Church in the preaching, where he won golden opinions. But less than six months after his marriage, the living of King's Nympton fell vacant by the death of Edmond Squire, the Rector, on August 6, 1620.

Martin Blake immediately presented himself to Bishop Cotton of Exeter for priest's orders, and was ordained priest by him on August 11, 1620. On the next day he was instituted to the Rectory of King's Nympton, on his father's presentation ;—the Bishop's register states by reason of a grant from Ludovic Pollard of King's Nympton, Esq. A journey was then made to King's Nympton, to see what would be required to fit the house for himself and wife, after which he took his wife down to Plymouth till the house was ready, and on April 5, 1621, took up his residence at King's Nympton Rectory, and entered on a cure of souls.

Of his work here there is little to be said ; it was the ordinary routine of a country parson of those and other days, though the hours have changed—morning prayer was said daily at 6 A.M., evening prayer at 3 P.M. The labourer on his way to work saw his parson going to the

The Life of Martin Blake B.D.

church and could join him.   Then there were the
sick and poor to be visited, and reading and
study for his B.D. degree.

Blake himself says he continued labouring in
his parish for about six years.   But from 1625 he
was very little at King's Nympton, the work there
being entrusted after that date to curates, and in
these we may mark the gradual change in Blake's
religious opinions.   His first curate was Germanus
Goldston, almost an extreme Puritan.   He was
afterwards at Chagford, in 1662, and signed the
declaration of conformity, but was afterwards
deprived for non-conformity.   The second curate
was James Smith, a most orthodox Churchman,
who eventually succeeded as Rector of King's
Nympton on Blake's resignation, July 17, 1639.
Smith became afterwards precentor and Canon of
Exeter; a tablet to his memory, erected by his
second wife, may still be seen in King's Nympton
Church.   Two only of Blake's children were born
at King's Nympton; the eldest, Mary, was born at
Barnstaple, baptized there February 10, 1621, and
buried there October 17, 1622; the next, Elizabeth, I find from an entry in King's Nympton
register, was born at King's Nympton, on Thursday, January 22, 1623, and baptized at Barnstaple
27th day next following.   Indeed a large part of his
time was spent at Barnstaple, where, as he says,
"my abode at that time mostly was."   In 1625 he

The Life of Martin Blake B.D.

seems to have been at Plymouth, the year his father was mayor, and here his eldest son, Nicholas, called after his grandfather, was probably baptized. From there he journeyed to Oxford to take his B.D. degree, December 14, 1626, as a ten-year man, after which his active connection with Barnstaple, which lasted nearly half a century began. But before entering on this, it will be necessary to describe somewhat the state of religious affairs in that town.

CHAPTER II

THE VICAR OF BARNSTAPLE AND THE LECTURERS

1626-1640

Religious life in Barnstaple — Eccentricities of former vicar—Alienates the people—The lecturers —Richard Smith—Quarrels with Trender—Letter to Archbishop Abbot — Archbishop sends a preacher — Cox appointed lecturer — Corporation look out for a successor for Trender — Blake selected—Crompton appointed lecturer—Trender dies—Blake becomes vicar—Rebuilds vicarage— Services in the Church—The Parish Church in 1630—Large number of communicants—Friendly relations with lecturer—Brownist lecturer at Pilton stirs up strife—Blake Rural Dean—Presents lecturers — Pulpit controversies — Conventicle preachers—Preacher disguised as bookseller— Jonathan Hanmer—Letters of Bishop Hall and Hanmer—Blake accused of Arminianism—Quarrel with Crompton—Recorder appointed arbitrator— Crompton leaves—The Canons of 1640—Blake's letter to Hakewill.

BEFORE Blake came to reside at Barnstaple, religious life had been in a most unsettled state there for many years—it might be said ever since the beginning of the reign of Elizabeth.

The Life of Martin Blake B.D.

John Claris, who had been presented in 1562, was a priest who had been brought up in the pre-Reformation school, and was by no means in sympathy with the religious changes made at that time. A celibate, he lived in the little vicarage built as far back as the days of Bishop Stapledon, on the edge of the convent ground. As time went on he found himself more and more out of sympathy with his parishioners, and opposed to the lay control over Church affairs which the Mayor and Corporation were gradually acquiring; finally, he had come into conflict with the ecclesiastical courts, and was excommunicated at the close of the year 1589. He died 1590, having made a nuncupative will in favour of his servant. He was always styled in the old-time manner Sir John.

During his days, as in most of the country towns, Puritanism had made rapid strides, and a system of lectureships had grown up, the lecturer being appointed, paid, and dismissed, by the Corporation at their pleasure. The earliest regular lecturer was the Rev. Conan Bryan, Rector of Parracombe, who had a regular stipend paid by the Corporation as weekly lecturer.

On the death of Sir John Claris, Richard Baylie was instituted, but he only held the living for a very short period, resigning it on obtaining the more valuable living of Bideford; he was

c

The Life of Martin Blake B.D.

succeeded by John Trender, who held the living for thirty-five years, a man of very different temperament, more like the clerk whom Chaucer describes as the Jolly Absalom than the staid and sober divine whom the burghers expected to instruct, reprove, and exhort them. Of a jovial temperament, his amusements were the pipe and tabor, and it was also whispered the bottle. Used as they had been to celibate clergy, the new vicar not only married, but married thrice, taking a fresh wife, each time within a few weeks of the former one's decease—an abomination unheard of for a cleric, who, they had learned, was to be the husband of one wife—not one at a time, as the modern gloss is. Certainly, by his eccentricities and disregard of all in authority, he had alienated all the more sober-minded of his parishioners, and a regular lecturer had become almost a necessity with men who had not dreamt of such a thing as separation. Richard Smith, who had been appointed by the Corporation as lecturer, was a man of some parts, although of somewhat extreme Puritan views. Between him and Trender quarrels soon broke out ; it ended in Smith being inhibited and the vicar getting his parish clerk, Robert Langdon, ordained as a permanent deacon to assist him. Matters were then patched up for a time : Smith conformed to the Bishop's requirements, and continued to act as lecturer till his

The Life of Martin Blake B.D.

death (February 5, 1610-11). On this the more moderate men on the Corporation decided to get matters for the future placed on a more peaceable and permanent footing, and they decided to apply to the Archbishop of Canterbury to send them a lecturer with his authority, as they felt that Bishop Cotton of Exeter was altogether unsympathetic to them and their needs.

George Abbot, who had then just succeeded to the throne of Canterbury, was a man well known for his decided Calvinistic opinions, and it was considered that a man sent direct by the Archbishop would not only have a better ecclesiastical position, but also, from Abbot's views, sure to be acceptable to the more Puritanically minded. Accordingly the following letter was drawn up and sent to the Archbishop :—

"Right Reverend Father in God, the general care of this whole Church worthilie devolved upon your Grace and in regard of yor singular zeale for the religion of God and furnishing his harvest wth sufficient labourers so universallie applauded, emboldens us the poore inhabitants of Barnstaple in the Countie of Devon to become humble petitioners unto yor Grace. Who being of late for o^r sins by the hand of God bereaved of o^r painful and learned preacher Mr Richard Smith and having small hope among so many discouragem^{ts} any other way to repaire o^r

35

greevous losse doe therefore beseech yor Grace in commiseration of o^r distressed estates to commend unto us some grave and discreet Preacher, who not onlie by his learning may informe us in the mysteries of Christ's Gospel and defend it against the quarrels of the adversarie, but also by his godlie and exemplarie life may both tread and beate the path before us and stop the mouth of malicious slanderers. And although o^r means upon whom the stipend principallie must rest be but meane as being more willing than able, and the best able being not the most willing, yet we trust all will be so respective of one recommended by yor Grace as it may amount unto a competent proportion. And happilie the partie whom yor Grace shall send be desirous to take some experience of us before he resolve to settle amongst us, in the meane season we shall give him o^r best entertainm^t, and defray all charges both of comming and going. But we hope no dislike on either side shall arise ; and as we shall give contentm^t and securitie for what we promise, so we shall againe receive instruction and comfort unto o^r soules. Which obtaining by yor Graces meanes we yor graces humble petitioners shall become humble orators unto God for yor Grace that as he hath advanced yo^u unto the highest dignitie in his Church militant on earth and furnished yo^u with a measure of spirit proportionable thereunto, so he would also be pleased to reserve for yor Grace an eminent degree of glorie in his Church triumphing in heaven.

" From Barnestaple May 10 anno 1611
"Yo^r Graces in all humbleness
" to be commanded

" JOHN HANMER.

" JOHN DELBRIDGE.   WILLIAM PALMER, Jr.
" NICHOLAS DOWNE.   GEORGE BAKER, Sr."

The signatories to this letter were all the leading men of the Corporation. William Palmer, Jr., was Mayor in 1612, Nicholas Downe, 1613, John Delbridge, afterwards Blake's father-in-law, in 1600 and 1615, George Baker in 1616, John Hanmer, father of Rev. Jonathan Hanmer, in 1624.

In response to this letter a Mr Rawlinson was sent as preacher by Archbishop Abbot. He arrived accompanied by a chaplain and an apparitor of the Archbishop, to give every outward evidence that he was the accredited representative of the Primate of all England. He was enthusiastically received by the town, and an entertainment was given by the Corporation and a purse of gold presented to him ; but a short trial proved that he was not a sufficiently hot gospeller for the Puritanically minded, and after the enthusiasm had worn off was coldly treated

The Life of Martin Blake B.D.

and soon retired. Following him came William Handcock, who died almost immediately; then a succession of nine, running lecturers as they were called, none of whom pleased, till 1620, when Benjamin Cox appeared on the scene, and was ultimately appointed lecturer by the Corporation at the then handsome salary of £50 per annum, and it was to this appointment of Cox that Blake traced all the troubles that afterwards arose.

Trender was old and failing : the lecturer did not interfere with him, for in the regular services he had the assistance of his deacon-clerk, Robert Langdon, who died July 5, 1625, and was succeeded, both as a permanent deacon-curate and parish clerk, by Anthony Baker, an appointment that was agreeable to the Corporation, who presented Mr Baker with a set of robes. So Trender had assented to the appointment of Cox as lecturer for a term of three years.

At this juncture the thoughts of both orthodox and Puritan were turned to the question of who would succeed Mr Trender as vicar, and the thoughts of both parties turned to Martin Blake; both thought he would be exactly the man they wanted, and overtures were opened with Blake through his father-in-law, who had acquired the next presentation, as to whether he would accept the living when vacant if offered to him.

Blake knew something of the past history of

The Life of Martin Blake B.D.

the parish, and was by no means desirous of undertaking the position, but it was represented to him that his accepting would be the means of healing the dissentions that had long vexed the Church at Barnstaple. Blake pleaded that he could not afford to give up his Rectory for the poorly endowed vicarage of Barnstaple; but it was pointed out to him that there would be no need of his resigning King's Nympton, as that matter could be arranged with the Bishop, so at last, after frequent conferences with Dr Hakewill and Rev. John Downe, Blake consented, as he says, "at the great importunity of my father-in-law, Mr John Delbridge, and many other my well-wishing friends."

John Trender, "the ancient vicar," died November 17, 1627; but shortly before this Benjamin Cox, whose term as lecturer had been further extended, accepted the perpetual curacy of Sandford, near Crediton, and a Mr William Crompton, of Brasenose College, Oxford, had been appointed as his successor, with the consent of Mr Trender.

On the news of the death of Mr Trender reaching Blake, he went to Exeter and had a long interview with the new Bishop, Dr Joseph Hall, a man of singular piety and learning, and taken then to be rather a favourer of the Puritans, though it was his lot before he died to be an

The Life of Martin Blake B.D.

example of constancy to the principles of the Church in times of its persecution. By Hall's advice Blake determined to accept the vacant vicarage, and was instituted December 1, 1628, on the presentation of his father-in-law, John Delbridge, and on December 6 he arrived at Barnstaple, where, as he says, he " received much contentm' from the love of the people in their zeal (as I then looked upon it) in the things of God, and their loving acceptance of me and my endeavours."

He found, however, the vicarage house totally unfitted for his family, and almost a ruin ; the old house first built by the monks of the Priory in the Maudlin Close at Bishop Stapeldon's order had always been a small and ill-designed building, and hitherto no family had ever lived in it. Till Trender no vicar had married ; and though Trender had married three times, taking in each case a fresh wife within a few weeks of his old one's decease, there had been no children, and latterly the vicarage had been almost uncared for. Blake writes, in a letter to his Bishop, " that on his arrival he found the vicarage no better than a ruinous heap, and that he had to expend at once more than £300 (a large sum for its repair in those days), and had to build anew from the ground."—(Letter to Bp. Hall, dated October 4, 1639).

THE VICARAGE, BARNSTAPLE

The Life of Martin Blake B.D.

Towards this outlay the Corporation lent Blake £100 (Borough Accounts, 1629-30), which the vicar repaid them in 1636.

The vicarage rebuilt by Blake with the outer wall to the street is substantially the vicarage as we see it now. The stone mullions of the windows have been replaced by wood; and in the early nineteenth century the Rev. H. Luxmoore inserted a new window over the porch, with battlements above and a large bow window, all in the Churchwarden Gothic of that period; but otherwise the front to the street is exactly as it was built by Blake, and is a good example of the domestic architecture of the period. The interior, however, has been somewhat remodelled, though some interesting old plaster-work still remains.

Blake's first year as Vicar of Barnstaple must have been a sad and anxious time to him: besides having to build a new vicarage, sickness was rife in the town; over thirty were buried the first month of his incumbency. Among the victims was his sister-in-law. His daughter Agnes died the following March, and his father, owing to the large sums he had advanced when Mayor of Plymouth for the Cadiz Expedition, was in sad financial straits. Much of his time was occupied in the pastoral visitation of his sick and dying parishioners, but his first care was to revive and set in order the daily offices of the Church : morning prayer was said regularly at 6 A.M. ; at 11 a lecture or reading of scripture was given ; at 3 P.M. evening prayer was said.

The lecturer, Mr William Crompton, a man of some attainments, found that the new vicar was ready to accept him as a coadjutor, and he on his side welcomed the vicar's friendly advices ; and so, as Blake says, "a great league of friendship (as I conceived) was contracted between Mr Crompton and myself." Barnstaple seemed to have returned once more to the days when men were of one accord in the house. It is somewhat difficult to picture Barnstaple Parish Church and its services in the days of Martin Blake, for materials on this point are very scanty. Save for a few stray leaves among the Borough Records, there are no Churchwardens' accounts before 1729 [even that book has now disappeared] ; and the barbarous restorations of 1811 and 1825, which swept away the arcades, the worked stonepillars, the pointed arches, the carved and painted screens, and turned an ancient Gothic church into a semi - Egyptian temple crammed with seats and galleries, makes it very difficult to reconstruct the church as it appeared in early Caroline days. But in Blake's early days the building still retained most of its pre-Reformation features : the rood had gone, but the

The Life of Martin Blake B.D.

screen and rood loft still remained, with a dormer-window in the nave roof to light it; the Mayor's or Maister's Aisle, as the north transept was called, was separated from the rest of the church by carved oak screens, and its roof was a flat panel one, enriched with colouring; the walls had few monuments (most of the fine ones which are the glory of the church now were erected during Blake's incumbency), but were covered with inscriptions and texts in large black letters, which had replaced the older frescoes in 1592; seats were still not numerous in the church. In Blake's monument we see the congregation standing; but just twenty years before Blake's coming oak benches to seat 120 had been fixed; previous to this, except for the seats of the clergy, clerk, and "helpers of the quere" in the chancel, and the dignitaries of the town in the maisters' aisle, there were only the sieges or seats belonging to individuals who had purchased a right to the same for their lives.

On Blake coming to the parish, the only services he found, after the years of neglect by old Vicar Trender, was: morning prayer, said daily at 7 A.M., by Anthony Baker, the parish-clerk, who was in deacon's orders; the lectures of the Corporation lecturer, William Crompton; and services on Sunday morning at 10 A.M., and in the afternoon at 3 P.M. There was also a certain

The Life of Martin Blake B.D.

amount of preaching at private conventicles, which Blake set himself to put down, as contrary to all order. Blake introduced, in addition to these, an early prayer at 6 A.M. and a lecture every morning; also, litany on Wednesday and Friday mornings and catechizing in the church on Sunday afternoon at 2 P.M.

The Holy Communion had been somewhat irregularly celebrated before Blake's coming, owing to Trender's age and neglect; but the vicar returned to a regular monthly celebration. The solemn preparation for this service is fully described in a small book of devotions used by a lady of Blake's congregation, an ancestress of my own. She says: "Before the Communion I prepare myself after this manner: some two days before I examine mine owne conscience; I humbly confess mee, and am heartily sorrie for my sinnes; when I may not fast, at the least I eat and drinke sparingly; the next morning I begin sooner than other times a prayer in my minde, therein desiring the Grace of God to communicate sincerely. Then I consider how great a thing it is to be partaker of so holy a mysterie, to receive Him whom the Angels adore, the Prophets have desired, the Apostles loved, the Martirs imitated, and all holy men coveted with unspeakable desire to honour, love, and unite them unto Him by this holy sacrament."

The Life of Martin Blake B.D.

The enormous number of communicants in Blake's time may be judged from his statement that it took two hours to simply communicate them, and so he revived the ancient custom at Barnstaple of the singing of psalms during the communion of the people, as being both edifying and convenient. But the principal service in the townsmen's mind was the State service on Sunday mornings. Every Sunday morning the Corporation assembled at the Guildhall, which stood at the High Cross and close to the west end of the church. Nowadays the Mayor is the only one who wears his scarlet gown, but in those days every member of the Corporation had on his election to provide himself with a gown, vested in which he walked with his brethern in solemn procession to the church, attended by the Seneschal (or Town-Clerk, as he is now called), Constables, and Sergeants-at-Mace, and took their seats in the Maister's Aisle. In those days fines were levied for non-attendance at their Parish Church on Sundays and Holy Days, but the very small number of those levied in Barnstaple, as compared with those in the records of many other Corporations, is evidence that Blake's ministrations were acceptable to the townsmen.

The vicar made a point of always preaching himself, when possible, at the service on the Sunday morning, to do honour to the authorities

The Life of Martin Blake B.D.

and dignitaries of the town, and from the lengthy and prolix manner of the worthy vicar in his writings, it is very probable that the hour-glass, which had been fixed to the pulpit as early as the year 1572, was not unfrequently turned over before the vicar had finished his discourse; for if the early seventeenth century was a period strong in controversial divinity, it was a period also of very earnest effort after a revival of spiritual life, and religion was a regular part of most men's daily life. And so things went pleasantly for a time, till the period of Mr. Crompton's appointment as lecturer was drawing to an end, when the Mayor and Corporation requested Blake to agree to him being reappointed lecturer for another five years. Blake expressed himself as agreeable, but no written agreement was signed, which Blake, in the light of after-events, always regretted; for the fly in the ointment soon appeared: the attendance at the 6 A.M. service suddenly diminished largely, and the vicar, on enquiry as to the reason, found that a certain John Can, the lecturer at Pilton Parish Church, a rigid Brownist (or Independant, as we say now), had infected a number of the Barnstaple parishioners with what Blake called the sour leaven of Brownism.

Can had never relished the Puritan Mr Crompton, but "especially his stomake rose

The Life of Martin Blake B.D.

against Blake ; " and so he not only railed against Barnstaple's vicar and his teaching from Pilton pulpit, but also caused little slips of paper, with the words " Take heed of your stinted morning prayer," to be thrust under the doors of all the attendants at Blake's early service, which led away some of the weaker members. Blake says : " The petulancy and strife of this wicked man having wrought so great distraction, I was forced at last to cry down his base carriages wherever I came ; " and the vicar so far prevailed that Can went off to Amsterdam, taking some of his followers with him. Others were only kept back from following him by Blake's persuasions, though it would have been far better had he let them go too ; for now that " the empty Can had gone to Amsterdam, the make-bales got hold of Mr Crompton, and persuaded him that Blake, as a pluralist, was unworthy of credence," and so a breach was made in the hitherto friendly relations of the vicar and lecturer, and at the end of 1629 a new subject of difference arose.

It had been the custom at Barnstaple Church from Elizabethan days for the choir to sing psalms during the administration of the Sacrament. During the latter part of Trender's vicariate, Crompton, to whom things had been mainly left, had dropped the custom at the request of some of the Puritanically minded ; but

47

The Life of Martin Blake B.D.

Blake, finding that with his large congregation nearly two hours were occupied in communicating his people, had, with the approval of the Mayor, revived the old custom, and this revival became an acute controversial point between them. Crompton contended that it was not ordered in the rubrics, and was unlawful. Blake justified it as an ancient and lawful custom, and more than that—very convenient in large congregations. It was a new position for one of the party noted for their nonconformity to plead strict conformity, and in this case decidedly unpopular, for the congregation were well pleased to enjoy their ancient custom ; so Crompton quickly yielded the point. But now another subject of difference arose. Blake, in accordance with the curious custom that prevailed till 1860, had been elected Rural Dean of Barnstaple Deanery as the "noviter inductus," and in that capacity received the following letter from Archdeacon Helyar :—

"To Mr Martine Blake, Vicar of Barnstaple, Deane Rurall of the Deanery of Barum for the yeere last past give these.

"Whereas of late there haue beene certaine orderes by the King's Matie, directed to the most reverend father in God the Lord, ArchB^{pp} of Canterbury, and from his grace to the right

The Life of Martin Blake B.D.

reverend father in God the Lord B^PP of this
diocese of Exeter, and from him to vs and from
vs to y^u concerninge the observance of Catechis-
inge in the afternoone on Sundayes (instead of
Sermons) by question and answer by the Minister
of every severall parishe within your Deanry.
And likewise for every Lecturer's observance of
readinge divine service accordinge to the Liturgie
printed by authority in his hoode and surplesse
before his lecture.   And also whether where
their is a Lecture sett up in any markett Towne
the Lectureres be grave and orthodoxe.   Divines
neere adioyninge to the same markett Townes
and of the same dioces and doe preach in their
gownes and not in cloakes.   And lastly yf a
Corporation doe mainteyne a single Lecturer
whether he the sayd Lecturer be suffred to
preach before he professe his willingnes to take
upon him a livinge with cure of Soules within
that corporation and actually to take such
benefice or cure soe soone as it shall be fayrely
procured for him.   These are to commaunde and
requier you that with all expedicion you make
diligent inquyry with the wardens and sidemen
of every particular parishe within your foresayd
Deanery (as well peculiars as otheres) whether
the sayd orderes have been punctually observed
or who hath transgressed the same.   And to
certifie unto vs at the next Court at Barnestaple

The Life of Martin Blake B.D.

vitz. the ninth day of December next the names and surnames of the severall offenders and the qualities of their offences in writing and that y^u appeare yourselfe at the same tyme that thereby you may give such full satifaccion to his Lo^{pp} in this behalfe as his Lo^{pp} expecteth and we are bound to performe and heerof we requier you to take speciall care and notice and soe we committ you to God and rest,

"Yo^r very loving friend

"WILLIAM HELYAR.

"EXON., 8 *Novemb.*,
   "1630."

In accordance with this, Blake felt himself bound to present some of the lecturers, Mr Crompton among them. This act of Blake's though merely an official return, gave mortal offence, not only to Crompton, but to the whole Puritan party in the deanery, they could not call him to account for an official act, but they henceforth looked on him as a traitor, and pretexts for differences in that age of theological controversies were quickly found, and Blake's fondness of arguments and his love of writing theses gave further opportunities.

First a controversy was started on the subject of original sin, whether the traduction of it from the parents to the children (as the very ὅτι of it)

could be proved by scripture evidence. This led to a pulpit controversy, Blake maintaining it could, Crompton that it could not. Second, a controversy arose as to the law and the Gospel, whether, that merely in the preaching and pressing thereof doth bring light enough to inform, and grace enough to convert a sinner to his salvation.

Blake preached an expository lecture every Wednesday evening on this subject, and in one of his lectures expressed the view that the preaching of the sentence of the Lawgiver against sin and sinners was not of itself sufficient to produce the gracious effect of conversion, but was a good preparation to qualify the subject for the offer of grace tendered in the Gospel.

Crompton lectured Sunday afternoons on the opposite side, and the Sunday after he quoted Blake's words and condemned the same for downright blasphemy against the law and word of God. Such passages as these did not make for friendly relationships, for both Blake and Crompton were very tenacious of their views, and the congregation were inclined to take sides; for in all ages, and in that one particularly, the layman was ready to consider himself as good a judge as the theologian on theological science; he will take his law and his medicine from the lawyer and physician unquestioning. Not so religious views; he thinks he knows as much on this subject as any Doctor of Divinity, and in the Blake and Crompton controversy many a Barnstaple parishioner considered his judgment on what was orthodox or heretical as good as his pastor's. However, in this one, Crompton at last, as Blake says, "did ungraciously retract his error as to this particular, and in so doing made amends both to the truth and me."

But to turn aside from these pulpit controversies, Blake's ministrations were in general acceptable to his parishioners, conformists and non-conformists alike, and as yet there was no open opposition worship, but secret preachings were beginning to be held by the extreme Puritans in private houses, with whom there was some trouble. Among these was a certain John Cole, who had a large following, consisting mainly of the lowest classes, serving-men and women, and such like, who flocked to his sermons, the teaching of which ran into every extravagance and anti-nomianism. The result was a fearful scandal, for he wrought the silly women to his lust, persuading them that their acts would stand for grace (" Cal. State Papers," Dom. Series, December 1624). It had gone on for two or three years in secret, till one of the women went to the vicar and made a confession which so horrified him that he laid it before the bishop, who opened a commission to

The Life of Martin Blake B.D.

search out the affair, and wrote to the Mayor, Alexander Horwood, an extreme Puritan himself, bidding him hold the villain Cole in prison.

The vicar had also his domestic worries. His father, Nicholas Blake of Plymouth, had been ruined by the heavy charges he had to incur while Mayor of Plymouth, and the sums he had advanced in connection with the Cadiz Expedition, and was imprisoned for debt. He petitioned piteously for payment, being then eighty years of age ("Worth's Plymouth," p. 218). On his release he left Plymouth and came to Barnstaple to join his son, the vicar ; his next surviving son, Nicholas, was already settled in Barnstaple with Mr Thomas Matthews, a Bilboa merchant, who had married Mrs Martin Blake's niece, Martha Ayer, and afterwards married their daughter Mary. (These relationships are somewhat puzzling, as Nicholas Blake, junior, married his brother's great-niece by marriage.)

The beginning of Blake's great rupture with the Puritan party started in 1633-4. In that year, Mr John Delbridge, the vicar's father-in-law, being Mayor, a bookseller and bookbinder was greatly needed in the town ; the choice of such a person required great care and consideration, for seditious books and tracts were plentiful and their circulation was a thing to be carefully guarded against. The Mayor and his son-in-law, the vicar, enquired of Bishop Hall of Exeter, as to whether he could recommend them a suitable person to admit into the town in such a capacity. The bishop advised them to engage Thomas Langford, an expert man in the trade ; but before the negotiations were concluded, Mr Delbridge's mayoralty ended, and he was succeeded by Alexander Horwood, an extreme Puritan, and one described as not altogether the wisest or best affected unto peace. Horwood, while outwardly continuing the negotiations with Langford, wrote also privately to a Puritan preacher in London, Mr Henry Burton, asking him to recommend them someone else. Burton proposed a certain Thomas Smith, and sent him down to Barnstaple, and at the next council meeting, Horwood proposed to admit Smith as the recognised bookseller in the town. Blake on hearing of this, and knowing that Smith was really a dissenting preacher in disguise, brought the matter before Bishop Hall, who wrote to the mayor, advising him of the danger which he feared would ensue on their choice of Smith, and earnestly entreating him to accept Langford ; but Horwood gave little attention to the Bishop's letter, and was more set on having Smith. The vicar, finding himself unable to prevent Smith's appointment, endeavoured to prevent some of the growing mischief he foresaw, and meeting Mr Horwood, the Mayor, with four others of the chief of his brethren in the street, he requested them to admit Langford and Smith together as partners, as Smith really knew nothing of the trade, while Langford was an expert. Horwood was opposed to this altogether; but the rest said they liked the idea well enough, and would do their best endeavour at the next meeting of their house to bring it into effect. On this, Horwood, though he would not promise to agree in formal words, was silent, and did not oppose it as he had done at first. Blake, having obtained this promise, hoped it would all be quietly settled by this compromise; but a few hours after, the mayor called his brethren of the Council to the Guildhall, proposed "that Langford should be excluded, and Smith only admitted to exercise the trade of book-selling and book-binding in this town," and carried his point. The vicar complained of breach of promise, but to no effect, Horwood contending that the vicar's proposal to make Smith and Langford partners was unreasonable, that Smith was a sanctified and godly man and Langford a carnal man, and there was no reason that two men so differently affected should be joined together in partnership. Horwood, however, owned privately that his real reason was, that if Smith was by himself he could freely sell what books he liked (whether they were books licensed or forbidden), but if Lang-

The Life of Martin Blake B.D.

ford was a partner, he could only sell books that were warranted by the public authorities, for fear lest Langford should discover him in so doing.

Smith, on settling himself in the town, soon showed himself a bitter sectarian and opponent of Blake, and lost no opportunity of sneering at the vicar's preaching, and ostentatiously every Sunday went off to some other parish with as many as he could collect. This nettled the vicar exceedingly, as he rather prided himself on his preaching, and, instead of maintaining a dignified silence, somewhat foolishly gave out as his text the following Sunday : " For ye are yet carnal :— for whereas there is among you envying and strife and divisions, are ye not carnal, and walk as men ? For while one saith I am of Paul ; and another I am of Apollos ; are ye not carnal ? " (1. Cor. iii. 3, 4), and proceeded to refer plainly to Smith and his followers. The following day Smith met the vicar in the High Street and challenged him for perverting the Apostle's words, and said he had spoken that which he could not justify, and that the vicar only went up into the pulpit to rail and make lie. " While the people of God here," said Smith, " saw grounds to believe that you were a downright godly man, they never left you ; but that now from your doctrine and conversation they see grounds to the contrary, they do indeed forsake you."

The Life of Martin Blake B.D

In private, afterwards, Smith boasted he had set the vicar down, and that Mr Horwood, the Mayor, would soon have Blake in the Star Chamber or High Commission Court. As for himself, he had the spirit of prayer, and therein had the advantage over all his opposites, being assured that God would refuse their prayers who were against him. Smith's extravagance, however, alienated the more sober part of the townsmen, and his trade fell rapidly to nothing. For a time he was supported by collections made for him all over the county by the extreme Puritan party, but in the end had to leave the town (though Mayor Horwood presented him with £20 from the Borough Funds on his leaving), when Langford was admitted to carry on the business in his place.

After Smith's departure religious affairs soon settled down again, Blake being on good terms with what may be called the High and Low Church parties in those days. Indeed, to understand Blake's position and troubles, it must be recognised that his quarrels and differences were not with those who were inclined to Puritanism, and who in after years during the civil war became practically Presbyterians, but with the party whose inclinations were with Independency,—the Brownists, as Blake calls them ; their views were the antithesis of Presbyterianism, and in Blake's first persecution it was only the clergy with

The Life of Martin Blake B.D.

independent sympathies, such as the three Downe's at Goodleigh, Northam, and Exeter, the Bartletts at Bideford and Fremington, and Hawkins of Filleigh, who were found opposing him. The other Puritan clergy and ministers of the neighbourhood, such as Anthony Palmer of Bratton, Leonard Prince of Ilfracombe, Jonathan Hanmer of Bishop's Tawton, William Clyde of Instow, John Berry of Landkey, and Lawrence Hatch of Marwood, although supporters of the Presbyterian system established in 1646, took no part whatever in the opposition to Blake ; on the other hand, they were more often found among his supporters.

The year 1634 marked the first prominent appearance in the religious life of Barnstaple of Jonathan Hanmer, afterwards so well known there, as mentioned before. He was the fourth child of John Hanmer, merchant of Barnstaple, by his marriage on February 20, 1592, with Sybel Downe. Jonathan Hanmer was born and baptized at Barnstaple on October 3, 1606, and had been educated at Emmanuel College, Cambridge, and ordained priest at St Margaret's Church, Westminster, in 1632, and immediately after presented to the living of Instow (March 27, 1633), vacant by the death of his uncle, the Rev. John Downe ; and at Blake's request he was appointed by Archdeacon Helyar to preach at his visitation, when his elocution and simplicity charmed and delighted his hearers. The following year Bishop Hall held his triennial visitation, and, on Blake's suggestion, requested Hanmer to preach again, in the following letter :—

To Mr Jonathan Hanmer, A.M., Rector of Instow, give these.

"SALUTEM IN CHRISTO,

"I have appointed my Triennial Visitation and intend (God willing) to visit in Person. I have made choice of you to preach at **Barnestaple** on Wednesday being the thirtieth day of March. I pray therefore prepare yourself to do it. In expectation whereof I sign myself

"Your loving friend and Diocesan

"JOS. EXON.

"FROM MY PLACE IN
     EXON, *Feb.* 13, 1635."

To this letter Hanmer sent the following answer :—

"MOST REVERENT DIOSCESAN,

"I received letters bearing date the 13th of February wherein your Lordship is pleas'd to injoin me to preach at your Personal Visitation at **Barnestaple** the 30th of March next. How willing I am to do your Lordship service, I wish I had wherein to make it appear. But how unworthy this way, both my years and abilities do plainly declare. My answer is requir'd by your Lordship which casteth itself into a Petitionary form. My humble suit unto your Lordship is, if not an absolute acquittance yet at least a reprieve for this time. I desire not a Quietus est (for your Lordship's commands shall ever find me a willing servant) only at present a Supersedeas. To promote which request of mine I shall entreat your L'dship to consider (omitting my present weakness and indisposition of Body) how many of my worthy Brethren in the Ministry there are whose shoulders are far more fit for this burden ; at whose feet it would become me to sit. And withal it is no longer since than the Archdeacon's last Visitation, that I (sed quam impar) was this way employ'd. I beseech your L'dship to pardon my boldness in this my plea. 'Tis the reasonableness of the request puts me into this course. I shall readily submit to your Lordship's determination and dispose of me, whether by a ratification or nullity of your Lordship's former injunction. This latter is much desir'd (if your Lordship so please) tho' the former shall not be declin'd (if my suit may not be granted) but have the utmost of my Endeavour.

    " For I am

        " Your Lordship's in all duty to be. commanded

           " JONATHAN HANMER."

The Life of Martin Blake B.D.

In the following year, another, and this time a more violent pulpit controversy began; it was started by a sermon which Blake preached on September 3, 1636, at the funeral of Raleigh Clapham, apothecary of Barnstaple, whose fine monument with effegies of himself, his wife, and nine children all kneeling, is one of the most conspicuous of the many stately monuments of this period which still adorn the Parish Church of Barnstaple.

Blake took as his text on this occasion the words: "He that believeth hath everlasting life," and spoke of the perpetuity of spiritual life—the life, he said, which God in this world is pleased to bestow on those whom He calleth according to His purpose; it is unnecessary to give extracts of his sermon. But Crompton, the next time he preached, accused Blake of preaching heresy and Arminianism. The five articles of the Remonstrants of Leyden had ever been to the Calvinists as a red rag to a bull, and anything that savoured at all of it was immediately girded at by them. Blake had very gradually emerged from the narrow doctrines of predestination in which he had been brought up. But the accusation of heresy was too much for him; he was most indignant as he said: "Suspicione heresiae oportet neminem esse patientem." And the quarrel grew, and Blake sought to terminate Crompton's engagement as

The Life of Martin Blake B.D.

lecturer; but this was treading on the corns of the Corporation's prerogative as nominators and paymasters of the lecturer. Hitherto the majority of that body had been Blake's supporters, but on this point they were against him. Crompton said he was engaged by the Corporation, and they, jealous of their powers, supported him. Blake, they said, had agreed to accept the term of five years, and therefore had no power to dismiss Crompton till the end of the term. There was no written agreement, but the original one between Trender and Cox was cited by the Corporation as being the terms under which Crompton had been reappointed. Blake pleaded that no appointment was valid without the Bishop's license and consent. At last it was agreed to leave the matter to the Bishop's decision, and accordingly the vicar, the lecturer, Mr Richard Beaple, the Mayor, Mr Richard Medford, senior alderman, and Mr Pentecost Doddrige, accompanied by the town-clerk, Mr Lane, journeyed to Exeter to lay each their sides of the question before the Bishop. In the borough accounts there are several notices of payments in connection with this—*e.g.*, £5 for Mr Mayor and his company, when Mr Blake caused them to be sent for by My Lord Bishop concerning Mr Crompton, 8s. 10d., for the town-clerk, etc. (Receiver's accounts, 1636-7).

Bishop Hall, in whom general trust seems to

have been placed, heard all parties; the whole question of the position of the lecturers at Barnstaple from the beginning was gone into; and at last the Bishop decided that the question between Blake and Crompton depended on a legal point which he was unable to decide, and which he directed should be referred to the deputy recorder of Barnstaple, James Welsh, Esq., and that the matter should be left to his arbitration. I have not been able to discover the exact terms of Mr Welsh's award, but the result was that **Crompton's** lectureship was ended; he retired to **Collumpton**, from which he was ejected in 1662 for non-conformity. Calamy says that on Crompton leaving Barnstaple, the town dwindled both in riches and piety.

At Crompton's departure, Robert **Liverland**, Curate of Mortehoe, was appointed lecturer, and remained till 1641.

I have dwelt at some length on Blake's conflicts with the lecturer, as it was the source of all the troubles that befell Blake in later times. But the eve of the great rebellion was now casting its shadow over the country, and destroying the last hope of religious peace by raising new points of difference; and perhaps the first rumble of the storm was the subject of the Canons of 1640. They became the subject of long debates in the House of Commons, and formed the chief ground

The Life of Martin Blake B.D.

of the impeachment of Archbishop Laud and other bishops. It was the 6th of these canons which imposed the famous " Et cetera " oath on all clergyman, physicians, proctors, schoolmasters, etc. The oath was so called from the et cetera which appeared in the middle of it, and was said to deny that the king was a governor of the Church, unless he was included in the word, "etc." —as someone said, a scandalous place for his majesty.

From the space which the consideration of the canons occupies in Sir John Northcote's "Note-book," we can see how this imposition of a new oath excited the feelings of clergy and laity alike. No oath, it was said, can be imposed but by parliament, and therein the canon was against Common Law. This being the common talk, it is not surprising to find that many of the clergy had scruples about taking it. Among the number was Martin Blake. Some correspondence seems to have passed between him and his brother-in-law, Dr George Hakewill, as to the lawfulness of taking it. The following letter from Blake to Hakewill explains Blake's views on this subject :—

" DEAR BROTHER,

"I have received your very loving and Christian letter with much comfort and content-ment of spirit, but am sorrie that as I was

burdened first abroad and since at home that I
could not with satisfaction to mine owne selfe
returne a speedier answer. I perceive by what I
have now learned of you that your mynd hath
been no less exercised with doubts and scruples
about this oath with the appurtenances thereto
than mine hath been. For myself I have desired
if I so could, how in this thing I might steer a
right course between command and conscience and
preserve obedience unto both but as yet can find no
satisfaction.

" At first I thought if the words might tolerably
be expounded at the tyme of taking this oath, we
might safely enough have undergone it and upon
this ground I began to think how the Articles of
the Church of England together with the Canons
which we have alreadie subscribed and according
to wch we have sworn canonical obedience doe
lay such faire grounds of explication to this oath,
that if our superiours would permit us in that
sense only to take the same and so record it our
scruples might have received good satisfaction.
Consequently upon this I thought againe that our
Reverend Diocesan (if in an humble way first
sought unto) would not be difficult to give us all
good contentment in the thing : especially, if we
would make it appeare unto him that the explication wch we would crave to be admitted was not
a fancie of our own but the comon Dictate of our

The Life of Martin Blake B.D.

Church, in her most warranted and best approved Rules. Upon these considerations I set myself a worke and proceeded a great way in the framing of such an explication according to these Rules with an intent to have presented them to our good Bishop, a copie of wch I herewith send you (among other Papers) to peruse. But when I had travelled thus far and in the end of my labour set myself to take a review of the whole, reflecting somewhat more seriously upon the binding part of the oath and particularly by that clause wherein it is required that we should ' Plainley and sincerely acknowledge and swear all these things according to the plain and comon sense and understanding of the same words.' I perceived plainer that my endeavours were all lost for that (in the taking of this oath) I am by this clause so tyed to the verry letter than an explication from the Giver or receiver of it may not be allowed : and yet without an explication who can take it ?

" Being thus disappointed of my first hope I knew not in the next place what to doe only casting myself into the Fatherly arms of Divine Providence. I did most heartily and humbly pray that God (of his great goodness) would so beare rule in the heart of our dear Soveraigne that either this oath might be wholly taken off or else explained by *Comon Authoritie* according to the tenor of those Articles and Canons where unto

The Life of Martin Blake B.D.

(by the comand of like Authoritie) we have already subscribed and from w^{ch} (under the generalitie and ambiguitie of words) we may not presume to varie or depart in the least degree especially seeing his Matie hath so far expressed himself that he will not endure it, as you may see totidem verbis in his printed Declaration before the Articles of Religion as they were reprinted anno 1628°. In the midst of these wishes and desires of mine wherein I doubt not many hundred did concur with me I heard of certaine Petitions this way tending, preferred, some unto his Matie: and some unto the Lords; and not long after of a new Sumons for another Parliament to whose wisdom and scaning (as I am creditably informed) his Matie hath sayd he will refer this new Oath together with the foregoing and following Canon in the same book.

[Here the MS. is much torn, so we give only final parts of this very lengthy letter.]

" Meanwhile dear Brother I cannot but returne unto you ample thankes as for the affectionatenesse of your love towards me every way, so especially for those frequent demonstrations of it in those christian and cordial encouragements wch partly by your pen and no less by your example and holy practice you give unto me in my poor labour for the Church. Surely no more than need: Corruption from within and opposition from

The Life of Martin Blake B.D.

without through the endeavour of a wicked
Devill in both doe draw after them discourage-
ments enough. But thankes be unto God we
have his promise and in that promise his whole
selfe his wisdome his strength and all as well as
love and mercie to stand by us and beare us up
if the heartie (though weak) endeavour of well
doing we shall unfainedly comit ourselves unto
him. Now our good God grant unto us his
faith and feare and multiply unto you (my dear
brother) his holy comforts! in the interim you
know his (euge :) is enough Discomfort may not
long rest in that blessed soule where this blessed
voice of his is heard. And I doubt not, but as
God hath set you in the way, so he hath brought
you within the sound too, in the contemplation
and fruition whereof I now leave you. And so
with mine and my wife's most heartie love
remembered to you and my good sister, with all
the rest of yours I commend you all to the grace
of God and ever am

" Your most affectionate and truly loving Brother,
     " MARTIN BLAKE.

" I pray when you have perused these enclosed
Papers return them to me againe for I have no
other copie of them.—Vale."

I have given this letter at almost full length as
a somewhat interesting example of the religious

The Life of Martin Blake B.D.

difficulties of one of the clergy and the private correspondence of Blake with a clerical connection; but I must now turn from the religious difficulties to the political troubles which followed so quick upon their heels, and in which Blake, though much against his inclination, became ultimately involved.

CHAPTER III

THE VICAR AND THE CIVIL WAR

1640-1646

George Peard—Thomas Matthews—Ship-money—
Blake refuses to pay his assessment—Convented
before the Bishop—His remonstrance—Council of
war—Vicar takes no part in politics—Desire for
peace—Declaration of Justices of the Peace for the
county—Suppressed by Peard—Blake gets a copy
of it—Conference of townsmen desiring peace—
Blake draws up considerations for a peace—Sends
it to the Council for War—Considerations ordered
to be burnt at the High Cross—Deputation to
Prince Maurice—Mayor, aldermen, and vicar's
letter to the prince—Surrender of Barnstaple—
Mayor's letter to Colonel Digby—Blake's letter to
Philip Francis, Mayor of Plymouth—Blake's
disappointment at renewal of war—Death of
Blake's wife and father—Keeps aloof during
Royalist occupation—Final surrender of Barnstaple.

AFTER the departure of Crompton, religious
matters in Barnstaple settled down quietly.
Blake's ministrations had always been acceptable
to the large majority, and as long as he kept
clear of pulpit controversies—of which he was

The Life of Martin Blake B.D.

somewhat fond—differences were unlikely to arise ; and, connected as he was, by marriage, with all the leading men of the Corporation, as the Delbridges, Downes, Doddridges, Ferrises, and others, he might, in general, reckon on their support. But a new influence was now rising in the town. George Peard, the eldest son of John Peard of Barnstaple, was a year younger than the vicar. He had been bred to the law, being a member of the Middle Temple, and was now a lawyer of some standing and good repute in his profession, and had been appointed Deputy Recorder of Barnstaple. A keen politician, he considered that his native town would afford him an opportunity of entering parliament and taking a prominent part in the nation's affairs, as it was well known that old Mr John Delbridge, Blake's father-in-law, who had been the town's representative since 1621, was anxious to retire, and Sir Alexander St John, the other representative, was unlikely to stand for Barnstaple again. Peard accordingly took up his residence in Barnstaple, and by his abilities and powers of oratory, soon acquired a commanding position. His residence in London had made him a firm opponent of the king and Laud, and his religious views were strongly tinged with Puritanism. The levying of ship money had touched the pockets of the Barnstaple merchants, and

71

The Life of Martin Blake B.D.

increased the feeling against the king. In 1639 some of the leading men in the town refused to pay their assessment, and Martin Blake, who was assessed at 15s., was returned among the number of defaulters, and ordered to appear before Bishop Hall. He replied that he would appear accordingly and render the reason of his refusal (Cal., " State Papers," Dom. series, 1639).

On October 8, 1639, Bishop Hall wrote to Sir Dudley Carlton : " I have just received an order to convent one of my clergy Mr Blake Vicar of Barnstaple and to receive his answer concerning his refusal of the payment of the shipping money which I have accordingly done and have here enclosed sent you his answer too full and prolix. You may be pleased to cut off the latter part which is too personal and to take notice of the real satisfaction he has given to this point. The man is peaceable and conformable and of more than ordinary desert let him speak for the rest for himself in his large answer. The enclosure is entitled,

" Remonstrance of Martin Blake Vicar of
Barnstaple to Bishop Hall of Exeter."

" In it he contends that the payment of the assessment does not pertain to the Vicar but to the impropriator of the place in proof of which he

The Life of Martin Blake B.D.

encloses an extract of the register which concerns an ancient Taxation of the Vicarage by Bishop Stapledon in 1311. He has forborne to pay the assessment of 15s. not out of a base desire to spare his purse, much less out of a refractory and perverse spirit against authority, but merely out of an obligation in conscience to preserve the right of the Church against the Impropriator, seeing the poor vicar's allowance is so small and also that his own expenses in the re-edification of the vicarage which was no better than a ruinous heap." Dated October 4, 1639.

In this year also, Blake lost his great supporter in the town by the death of his father-in-law, John Delbridge (buried June 26, 1639); but the accession of fortune that came to him by this, enabled him to resign the Rectory of King's Nympton, and he had always felt the imputation of being a pluralist, and was glad of the opportunity. But in 1640 Benjamin Cox, the old lecturer, was back in Barnstaple. He had got into trouble at Sandford by a furious sermon against all bishops, which even the tolerant Bishop Hall had to take notice of. Cox was summoned before him, but refused to retract or admit anything, and the bishop reported him to Archbishop Laud, writing :—" I am the more surprised at Mr Cox's conduct inasmuch as he had been one of the first of the clergy in my diocese to place the holy table altarwise." Cox was deprived and retired to Barnstaple a bitter opponent of the Church as it was, and though not a lecturer at the Parish Church, commenced preaching in conventicles, and fomenting discontent with the vicar as a conformist. To silence him Blake found impossible. Bishop Hall left for Norwich in 1641, and his successor, Bishop Brownrigg, never succeeded in establishing any authority in the diocese.

At the election of members of the Short Parliament in 1640, Blake's nephew, Thomas Matthews, was returned as member in place of Mr John Delbridge, but with George Peard; but in the November following, at the election of the Long Parliament, Matthews was replaced by Richard Ferris, a moderate parliamentarian, though a friend and connection of Blake's. But Peard's influence in the town was now commanding and it began to arm for the conflict. In 1642, Peard, who had taken a prominent part in the proceedings of parliament, obtained leave of absence to stay at Barnstaple for the service of that town and county (" Journal H. Commons," ii., p. 821). But Blake took no part or lot in politics; whatever his opinions were he kept them to himself. His nephew, Thomas Matthews, was the leading royalist in the town, but some of Blake's staunchest supporters were parliament

The Life of Martin Blake B.D.

men, and assisting its cause with voice and money. Barnstaple was fortified and held for the parliament. The tide of battle swept along with varying fortune in the west, and men began to realize what war really meant. Some found they had only exchanged one tyranny for another. The exactions of each party as they got the upper hand for a war levy, were enormous. The majority were utterly tired of the war, and if they could have peace, cared not which side had the better. Amongst this party was the Vicar of Barnstaple; the desire for a restoration of peace was the burden of many of his sermons during the war fever.

In the early summer of 1643, after the defeats of the Parliamentary forces in Devon, and the news of the entry of a new Royalist army into the county under Prince Maurice, the cause of the Parliament seemed to Barnstaple folk, with their limited horizon, hopeless. At the end of June, the leaders of the Royalist forces and the Justices of the Peace for the county issued the following declaration from Crediton, where they were quartered. As this document is, I believe, unknown (certainly it was unknown to Cotton), and has material bearing on Blake's life, I give it in full :—

" The Declaration of the Commanders and

The Life of Martin Blake B.D.

Justices of the Peace of ye Countie of Devon now in his Majesties Army."

"That although we are assured of his Maties readiness to give any assurances that his good subjects can desire, concerning the sinceritie of his pious resolution to maintaine the Protestant Religion, the just privileges of Parliament, the Libertie and Propertie of the subject, the Law, Peace, and Prosperitie of the Kingdome with such provision to be made as the Parliament shall advize for the ease of tender consciences in the reformation of Church government and Liturgie, and for the rooting out of Poperie wth such further acts of grace as can be any way beneficiall to his subjects and not destructive to his just perogative, yet notwthstanding some for their private ends and interests do contrive and continue to themselves an arbitrarie power (against Law) over the person and estates of their Neighboures and fellow subjects and to enrich themselves by the spoile of such as shall oppose their lawless humours and ambitions; do upon pretence that his Matie and those (who according to their allegeance adhere to him) intend to subvert religion Lawes and Parliaments, endeavour under colour of defending these to engage the Kingdome in a civill Warr, whereby they have removed (the only troublesome rub in the way) the Law,

76

The Life of Martin Blake B.D.

and brought all things to an extremitie and necessitie, and would now make that extremitie and necessitie (of their own making) the reason and warrant for their next actions, seaven times worse and more oppressing than the former, having hereby, of a happy flourishing Kingdome governed by Law, made us a miserable people regulated (as far as in them lyes) by meer will and power. Wherefore for ye removing of these scandalls cast on his Matie and ourselves, and for ye freeing of our fellow subjects from those illegal pressures and taxes they are now under, and for saving of both Counties and the whole Kingdome from ruine and to the end that it may truly appeare who are the enemies to Peace and Truth, wch only can reduce us to our former happie condition : We renouncing all private ends (other than the fruition of the blessed fruites of Peace in ye pursuit of it) doe declare and testifie to all the world, and are readie to give the strongest proofs that can be in reason desired. That our intentions are to defend ye true Protestant Religion against all Poperie and Schisme, his Maties person honour and estate, the just privilege of Parliament, the Libertie and Propertie of our fellow subjects (who shall concurr with us in a just peace) against all illegall imprisonments and taxes whatsoever. And, as for all such of the Justices, Gentlemen, and Freeholders of Devon as are desirous of

The Life of Martin Blake B.D.

peace with securitie of Religion, Lawes and Liberties, and a generall Pardon for all past offences by reason of the Warr, will meet and conclude on some forme of agreement between both Counties, we shall both secure their meeting and joyne with them in a petition to his Matie and both Houses of Parliament for their approbation of such good agreement as shall then be prepared for freeing of both Counties from such farther charges and ruine as Warr and their back wardness to Peace may otherwise produce.

" Jo. Berkeley.

" Jo. Heale.

" Edw. Seymour.

" Jo. Acland.

" Stoke, *Junij* 26°, 1643°."

This declaration was ordered to be sent about and published in every Parish Church in Devon, and the constables of every hundred were by warrants required to circulate it, and to give notice that the day appointed for the meeting was July 3.

This proclamation on coming into the hands of the Council of War at Barnstaple was promptly suppressed by the advice of George Peard, and many of the Royalist leaders in the county were not particularly anxious that it should be circulated there, for Peard by his zeal for the Parlia-

The Life of Martin Blake B.D.

mentary cause, both in Parliament and Barnstaple, had made himself particularly obnoxious to them, and, confident of their success, were not desirous of Peard and his friends sharing in a general amnesty.   A copy of it had, however, been sent by a friend at headquarters to Mr Thomas Matthews, who showed it to Mr Thomas Dennis, another leading Royalist in the town, and his uncle, the vicar, and asked their opinions.   He said the matter was instant.   July 3 was close at hand ; there was no possibility of a town meeting ; yet the proposals were such as even the Parliamentary men (except a few extreme ones) could agree to.   The vicar observed that it was a peace which he thought every moderate man could subscribe to, and it was decided that they should draw up their opinions in a form, communicate it to all likely sympathisers, and get them to sign it, and then forward it to the Mayor and Council of War, and ask them to call a general town meeting to consider it.   The following document was then drawn up, in which the hand of the vicar may be readily recognised.

" To the Wor^{sll} the Mayor of Barstaple as also to the worthy Gentlemen that are now of the Counsell of Warr there, the humble consideration of us the Inhabitants of ye sayd Town whose names are subscribed.

The Life of Martin Blake B.D.

"We hope it is not unknown unto you that Warr simply and in itselfe considered is not a thing to be delighted in. For besides that it goes attended with many other evills, it is inevitably destructive to the life of man wch we should studie to preserve. And if this be true of all Warr in the generall it may be much more revivified of civill War in speciall, w^{ch} (as Sir Benjamin Ruddierd[1] well said awhile since in the House of Commons) is like a two-edged sword, that cutts on both sides. Now, it is cleer to every eye that will but see, that such a Warr of late tymes hath mightily raged, as in other parts of the Kingdome, so in these two Counties of Devon and Cornwall, and hath alreadie gone attended with the destruction of many, whose deaths we cannot but bewaile, and (unlesse seasonably stopped) will certainly draw on, not only farther charges, to the utter impoverishing of our estates ; but more and more bloodshed, to the totall and fatall ruine of this late glorious Kingdome. Upon these considerations, it must needs be granted, that Christians especially (and so we among the rest) doe stand bound by all lawes both of God and Man to studie (as much as in them lyes) the prevention of these mischiefes, that they may not

[1] Sir Benjamin Rudyard, the member for Wilton, called for his eloquence the Silver Trumpet, was one of the secluded members in 1648.

80

The Life of Martin Blake B.D.

light or rest upon them : saving alwayes the preservation of Truth and Righteousnes, wch can only make our Peace happie. And, toward the furthering of this so pious and good a worke, that Partie wch first moves hath ye greatest praise, and (however things fall out) shall have the greatest comfort in the end. To this purpose therefore, it would be considered, whether (as things now stand) it would not become us (as our Saviour intimateth in that parabolicall expression, Luke xiv. 31) even without delay to make choice of some fit men from among ourselves to be imployed in a message to those Gentlemen who command over the kings forces in these westerne parts, to conferr with them about some good and honourable accord. And if so, then the message (though in other or more words) may for the substance of it be to this effect, viz.

" A message humbly proposed to be sent to the Counsell of Warr to be considered of, and (if approved by them) to be sent to the Commanders over his ^{Ma}^{ties} Forces in these Westerne Parts.

" NOBLE GENTLEMEN,
"Although through the default of some (whoever we know not thereof), your Declaration lately sent abroad from Crediton came not in any season ; nor indeed at all (to this very houre) in

The Life of Martin Blake B.D.

any orderly way, to take notice of it : yet now of late we have had the sight and perusall thereof to the full. In it you begin with an expression of your just confidence touching his Maties sincere and pious resolution to maintaine those good things, wch in the desire of all good men not only are but ought to be unanimously insisted on : as also his readines to give any assurance that his good subjects can desire in that regard. And then, after a few words interserted (wch in discretion and charitie, even for peace sake, we now wave), you goe on to a full and serious Protestation of the realitie of your own intentions to maintaine and defend the sayd things, viz., the true Protestant Religion, against all Poperie and Schisme ; his Maties Person, honour, and estate ; the just Priviledges of Parliament ; the Libertie and Propertie of the subject, against all illegall imprisonments and taxes whatsoever ; together with the Lawes of the Land : and hereof (you say) you are also readie to give unto the world the strongest assurance that can be in reason desired. These things thus premised, in the close of all we finde (as from you), a friendly invitation to the Justices, Gentlemen, and Freeholders of this Countie (who are desirous of Peace, with securitie of Religion, Lawes and Libertie) to meet and conclude on some forme of agreement between these neighbouring counties, together with a promise (on your parts) both to secure their meeting, and to joyne with them in a Petition to his Matie and both Houses of Parliament, for their approbation of such good agrement as shalbe then proposed for freeing of these Counties from such farther charges and ruine, as Warr and backwardnes to Peace may otherwise produce.

"Now, we hope that these things were by you no lesse sincerely meant, than they were freely uttered ; and that you wilbe as reall in performing, as you were forward in promising. And if so, then truely we cannot but expect that, though we did not (indeed we could not) come and confer with you at the tyme and place ; yet the failing in that circumstance hath not so farr altered the state of things, but that, in order to compass the same ends, we may confer still. There shall be (through[1] . . . . in us. For, whatsoever some men may (peradventure) thinke[1] . . . . the contrarie, yet We (who are most privie to our owne thoughts), do declare to you and to the world, that nothing can be unto us more comfortable than upon such termes (if rightly understood and meant), a heartie Peace. And accordingly we are and shall be readie to contribute our best endevours to so good a worke. Upon this ground it is, that, even now (in the midd'st of so

[1] MS. torn.

great heate), we have thus farr thought fit to declare ourselves, and to endevour (if possible) a good agreem^t for the generall welfare, as by the Propositions herewith sent unto you may appeare. Consider them, and give us to understand how you resent them. In expectation whereof, we rest as we ought, however you esteeme us,

"Your loving Frends.

"The Propositions, w^{ch} (if approved) may be likewise sent wth the foregoing Message.

"1. We desire to know of you, whether in truth and in realitie you doe constantly persist in your intentions to defend those maine things, wch in your late Declariton sent out from Crediton you seemed wholy to insist upon, viz. the true Protestant Religion, against all Poperie and Schisme ; his Ma^{ttes} Person, honour, and estate ; the just Priviledges of Parliament ; the Libertie and Propertie of the subject, against all illegall imprisonments and taxes whatsoever ; together wth ye Lawes of ye Land ?

"2. If so, then we propound unto you, that, because our desire is not to neglect our Neighbours (who are in association with us) but to take them along with us in a treatie of Peace, that so they as well as we may both vote in it, and injoy the benefit and fruit of it, there may be (for the tyme) a mutuall cessation of hostilitie

throughout these two Counties of Devon and
Cornwall, and so a free passage opened unto us
to meet and confer with our foresayd Frends,
about some fitting considerations for the shutting
up of these intestine broiles.   And the considerations, wch for the present we (for our parts)
doe reflect upon, may be these.

"(1) Let the particulars forenamed, and pretended on both sides to be stood for, be
so clearly expressed and set down, that in
the understanding thereof no scruple may
remaine, through the ambiguitie of words.

"(2) This done, and each Partie yielding full
assent unto the particulars so explaned,
let there be an assurance given (so farr as
in reason and religion it may and ought
to be desired on both sides) that the
intention is r . . . .[1] stant on all
hands, for the defence and maintenance[1]
. . . .

"(3) Upon this assurance mutually so given,
you may prese[1] . . . forces from us, and we
may retaine still the forces we have,[1] . . .
defend the forenamed particulars (wherein
we all agree) aga[1] . . . shall come against
us to infringe the same.   And, in case
either You[1] . . . in danger to be over-
borne by such unjust Opposers, let us

[1] MS. torn.

mutually ob[1] . . . ourselves in the strictest bonds of association, to come in to the assistance each of other, for the preservation of the common cause.

"(4) To the end this proposall of things for a good agreem[t] may take place, and be established among us, and consequently give encouragem[t] to others to follow our example, for the procuring of a more generall good : let there be a concurrence both of you and us in an humble and submissive Petition to his Ma[tie] and to the two Houses of Parliament, for their approbation of the Premisses.

"(5) That, when these great matters shalbe thus setled, all other differences may be likewise happily compounded, and therehence an universall Peace may follow, let it be carefully remembred, that in our sayd Petition to his Ma[tie] and the two Houses there may be some clauses importing our humble instant and joynt desire, both of a Nationall and free Synod, to settle good Orders in the Church ; and of a cordiall-christian Treatie, to rectifie distempers in the State ; and that all these may be concluded and shut up with an act of oblivion for all that is past on either side.

[1] MS. torn.

The Life of Martin Blake B.D.

"The Conclusion to Mr Mayor and the rest.

" And this Gentlemen in a way of humilitie and (as we hope) without offence seeing we presume not to prescribe or dictate anything to your Wisedomes, we have thought good to represent unto you our own deepest apprehensions towards the discharge of our dueties in these tymes of danger for the common good. We conceive ourselves in conscience bound to doe no lesse and we humbly entreate you to consider speedily and effectually of what we say. The God of Wisedome direct you!

"Subscribed with 36 hands men (for the most part) of prime ranke and qualitie of the Town and so presented to ye Counsell of Warr. Aug. 16°, 1643°."

The names of the signatories are not mentioned; they doubtless included, besides the vicar and Mr Thomas Matthews, Nicholas Dennis, Thomas Dennis, John Downe, Lewis Palmer, Edward Pointz, and other leading Loyalists in the town. The document was forwarded to the Council of War, and on the motion of George Peard, was scornfully rejected and ordered to be burnt at the High Cross by the hand of the hangman.

Peard could carry the Council of War with him, but a large number of the Corporation were of another mind. Opportunities to come to terms

The Life of Martin Blake B.D.

had already been let slip, and they would have to surrender and lose them all, and a copy of Prince Maurice's proclamation under his own hand was anxiously awaited. Days passed and none came; the lower classes thought they had been deluded by the vicar and his friends, and, as Blake says, our persons were in likelihood of some danger from the incensed multitude. The truth was, Prince Maurice's letter, sent by way of Colonel Digby, commander at Torrington, had been kept back by some, to whom Peard had rendered himself particularly obnoxious. The days passed, and nothing more was heard; so at a private meeting of those who had signed, it was agreed that Thomas Matthews should go at once to Exeter and see his friends at the Royalist head-quarters, and entreat them to solicit Prince Maurice for a further extension of time, and to obtain an invitation to submit, addressed direct to the Mayor and Corporation; and, at the same time, to order Colonel Digby to make no movement against the town till it had been considered.

Matthews was entirely successful in his embassy. He obtained a proclamation to the Mayor and Corporation signed by Prince Maurice on August 27, at Polsloe, and three days were given for an answer. This document is given in full by Cotton ("Civil War," pp. 213, 214), and so need

The Life of Martin Blake B.D.

not be printed here. With this Matthews rode
back post-haste to Barnstaple, and presented it
to the Mayor the next day (August 28, 1643).
The Mayor, William Palmer, at once called
together to the Town Hall all the burgesses,
both capital and common, and all who were rated
to the subsidies, excluding all others. The
Mayor then declared the business, read the
Prince's proposition, and invited opinions. Peard
at once rose and advised farther resistance.
London, he said, was still solid for Parliament,
and they must not judge of the state of things
in England generally, by their desperate position
in Barnstaple. Others expressed doubts and
scruples, which were eagerly explained away
by others, to the apparent satisfaction of the
doubters; and on the Mayor asking, Would they
assent to the terms? the answer came almost
unanimous, they would. Palmer then demanded,
Would they subscribe their names to the assent?
the answer again was, they would. The reply,
as given by Cotton ("Civil War," p. 215), was
then drawn up and signed by all the meeting,
with the exception of George Peard, Charles
Peard, William Nottle, and three or four others.
Cotton's copy of document had no signatures, so
I may state that the signatures were:—The
Mayor, William Palmer the Alderman, Martin
Blake the Vicar, and all the others present, and

The Life of Martin Blake B.D.

was despatched on Wednesday, August 30, to the Prince.

Although the Mayor's meeting was almost unanimous for surrender, there was a bit of disturbance in the town. The disbanded soldiers, sailors, and adventurers war had brought in its train, set on by the more furious schismatics and rabble, to use Blake's words, raised a tumult; "they beate up the drums, ran together in heapes, seized the fort, went up and downe by hundreds in the streets with their swords drawne, brake into some houses, and indeed caused many and great affrightments in the Towne." The Mayor with his officers went round ordering all to desist from their illegal and outrageous courses, and to go quietly to their houses. They paid, however, little attention to him and he had to retire from fear of personal violence. The next day, Thursday, the disorders were very little allayed, which caused Colonel Digby, to whom they were reported, to bring with him when he arrived on the Saturday to receive the Town's surrender a more considerable force than he had at first intended and to enter the Town (to use Blake's words) "though not in a hostile yet in a militarie" way, having first given a most strict charge to his men not to offer any abuse in word or deed to any inhabitant, which the soldiers to their great praise very honestly observed during the whole time of their remaining stay, which was about 8 or 9 days, at the end of which the town was left to itself, free from any garrison (according to the conditions agreed on), to be governed by the Mayor and his brethren.

To understand Blake's action in doing all he could to get the town to come to an agreement with the Royalist leaders, we must remember that what was in his mind was not a surrender, but a peace—a reconciliation of a divided house, —a peace that would be general all over England. And the following letter written by the Mayor to Colonel Digby and his officers at Torrington during the negotiations for the surrender shows that it was the idea entertained by those in the town who supported the surrender.

"Worthy Gentlemen,

"Your letter comming to our hands last night hath occasioned this answere from us now. And herein (with great contentment of mynde) we cannot but congratulate the free expression of your Christian ingenuitie, in being so willing to keep ye way plaine from those unkind rutts wch might else hinder a just Peace: a thing no lesse affectionately desired and pursued by us, than by them who love it most. To this end, also that we may satisfie your expectation, we doe hereby engage ourselves, to forbeare fortifying or acting any violence either upon you or your friends while the present treatie is on foot, the issue whereof (as we hopefully believe) will shortly appeare unto the world, in a blessed accord, to God's glory, the King's honour, and all our joy without wrong to any. This once accomplished our next hope is that your and our endeavours may so mutually concurr that (through the blessing of God) we may be successful instruments for the resettling of a good Peace throughout the Countie in a friendly way, wch is God's way and w^{ch} (we doe believe) is that you most love if to be had; and is unfainedly in the desire of us

"Your loving Friends, etc.

"(Blake MSS.)."

"Do not endanger our peace," were the words continually on Blake's lips during the three troublous days before the surrender, and on returning to his vicarage (on the evening of September 2, 1643, after it was accomplished) to meet his father, his first thought was still our peace: "May not our native town of Plymouth be brought into it as well as Barnstaple."

Accordingly two letters, in case one should miscarry, were written by Blake, and sent, one by Langford the bookseller and the other by another messenger, to Mr Philip Francis, the Mayor of Plymouth and others there beseeching them to join in the peace also. This action of Blake's, although entirely disinterested, was his afterward undoing; in Barnstaple his action was well understood and appreciated by both parties, but in Plymouth (which never surrendered) it led to his being identified with the Royalist party, and in after days was remembered against him.

The Royalist leaders had faithfully observed the terms of capitulation of Barnstaple, and had left George Peard and Charles Peard, the Mayor-elect, at liberty in the town; but Charles Peard on becoming Mayor raised great objections to the protestation issued in January by the Association of the Western Counties, and ordered to be delivered to all ministers of churches and chapels, and published the next Sunday during divine service. Blake willingly read the protestation and took the oath, but the Recorder and the Mayor fomented the opposition so as almost to raise an insurrection; it was nipped in the bud by the appearance of a troop of Prince Maurice's men, and owing to this breach of the agreement the town was occupied by a small military force, and the two Peards sent as prisoners to Exeter.

A great change, however, took place in the next few months in the fortunes of King and Parliament. In 1643 the rebellion in the west

The Life of Martin Blake B.D.

had almost collapsed, but in 1644, elsewhere, it was again in the ascendant, and Barnstaple, as the result of a plot engineered by Colonel John Lutterel of Santon, revolted to the Parliament at the end of June 1644. This state of affairs was, however, but short-lived. On September 27, it again surrendered to General Goring, and shortly after was strongly garrisoned for the King, Sir Allen Apsley being appointed Governor.

From then to April 1646, there is little to say of Blake's life. Disappointed in his hopes of a peace, he rigidly kept apart from all politics. Among his congregation part of this time was Prince Charles attended by his chaplain and tutor, Brian Duppa, Bishop of Chichester, and his retinue; but Blake, though a loyalist, was not a courtier—his heart was in theology, not politics. And during this period he devoted himself to literary work and published a treatise he had composed in opposition to some lectures of Benjamin Cox before the outbreak of hostilities. This treatise is entitled, " The Great Question so much insisted on by some touching Scandalous Christians as yet not legally convicted ; whether or no they may be lawfully admitted by the Minister or communicated with by the people at the Lord's Table. The affirmative maintained by way of answer to a discourse of Mr B. Cox, by Martin Blake, B.D., and V. of B. in Devon,

The Life of Martin Blake B.D.

London, 1645." During the Royalist occupation Blake had also another reason for keeping in privacy, as he lost both his wife and father, who were both buried in Barnstaple Church, on the south side of the chancel, near the Communion Table.

On April 14, 1646, the Royalist occupation of Barnstaple again came to an end, as after a short siege it surrendered to the Parliament under an Agreement. In No. 3 of these Articles of Capitulation it was stipulated—

"That no Clergiemen shall be questioned or accountable for any Act past or by them done or by any other by their procurement relating unto the unhappy differences between His Majestie and the Parliament . . . composition being made, they shall have indemnity for their persons and enjoy their estates and all other immunities."

CHAPTER IV

BLAKE'S FIRST PERSECUTION AND ITS END

1646-1648

The Committee for Plundered Ministers—The nine-handed petition against Blake—The vicar summoned before the County Committee—The town petitions in his favour—Appears before the Committee—Vicar suspended—Clerk alters sentence to sequestration — Blake's farewell letter to his parishioners—The plague at Barnstaple—No one to bury the dead—Letter to Sir John Bampfield—Tooker's second petition to Committee for Plundered Ministers—Blake sequestrated—Blake appeals to the Committee—Blake discharged—Tooker and Peard's fresh petition—Plundered Ministers Committee order case to be argued—Documents for the prosecution—Bradshaw's defence of Blake—Blake acquitted—Committee for county ordered to reinstate him—Sir John Northcote's letter

THE final surrender of Barnstaple and the pacification of the county of Devon brought into active operation the Act of Parliament for taking away the Book of Common Prayer, and for establishing and putting into execution the Directory, which had been passed on January 4, 1644-5, and again with slight alterations on March 5, 1645. Persons reading the Common Prayer Book thereafter were to pay £5 for a first offence, £10 for a second, and for a third to suffer a year's imprisonment without bail. Ministers neglecting to use the Directory were to pay 40s. for every neglect, and persons depraving the same, by speech or writing, to suffer a fine of not less than £5 or more than £50. All copies of the Common Prayer Book remaining in Parish Churches or chapels were to be carried by the churchwardens or constables to the respective County Committees to be disposed of as Parliament should direct.

But before Martin Blake could determine on what course of action he should take (though there is little doubt that, like most of the clergy with what we call Low Church leanings, he would have accepted the Directory, albeit somewhat unwillingly), another blow fell on him, for the change of masters brought also into active operation the standing Committee of the county for the sequestration of delinquents, as all who had in anyway actively opposed the Parliament were termed. And it was on the clergy that their hands fell heaviest, for the majority of them, whether high or low in their religious views, were mainly Loyalists ; and Blake, by the active part he had taken in what he had called the reconciliation of Barnstaple to the King, had forged a weapon

The Life of Martin Blake B.D.

which the few enemies he possessed were not slow to avail themselves of.

Immediately the news of the surrender reached London, two Barnstaple men, who had taken refuge in the metropolis during the last royalist occupation, drew up a petition against Blake, and presented it to the Committee of Parliament for Plundered Ministers, which had absorbed the powers of the Committee for Scandalous Ministers and other bodies. The petition was as follows :—

"Wee whose names are hereunto subscribed Inhabitants of the Towne of Barnestaple in Devon and Ministers wth others neare adjoyning do conceive and upon good grounds have just cause to believe that there will be no comfortable abiding in that Towne for Godly people who have been hearty in and left all for the publique cause if the now Vicar of Barnestaple, Mr Martin Blake continue in that place wth that interest as formerly, and the rather we are induced to beleeve this in regard that the said Mr Blake hath been a persecutor and opposer of Godly Ministers in that Towne and since these troubles hath very much complyed though in a very close and subtle way wth the enemies of God and the Kingdome and held intimate correspondency with some of the chiefest of them in all the times of his continuance in the Towne wth them, besides divers things w[ch] can be

The Life of Martin Blake B.D.

proved ag' him. Wherefore for the encouragement of the Godly and faithfull p'ᵗᵉ to the Parliament in that so considerable a Towne, and the
better carrying on the work of Reformacon in
that well affected corner of the Kingdome we do
humbly intreate this honble Committee that the
said Mr Blake according to his demeritts may
be removed from thence that an able and Godly
Ministry may be settled in that Towne wᶜʰ will
tend much to the glory of God, the furthering of
the work of Reformacon now in hand and the
great incouragem', comfort and satisfacion of the
hearty and godly partie in that Towne and pᵗᵉ
adjacent after all their very great losses and
sufferings.

" CHARLES PEARD. THOMAS DOWNE minister
" HUMPH. VENNER.   of Goodleigh neare Bar-
" EDWARD DYER.   staple.
" JO. TOOKER.   ANTHONY DOWNE minister
" BENJA. HAWKINS. of Northam neare Bar-
                   staple.
                   MARKE DOWNE minister.
                   JOHN HAWKINS minister.
                   WILLIAM BARTLETT
                   minister."

This is the petition which Blake so often in
his letters, and Walker after him, calls the nine-
handed petition, though it may be noted that

The Life of Martin Blake B.D.

there are ten signatures; probably it was that one of them was afterwards withdrawn. Only two of these, Peard and Tooker, were Barnstaple men; of the others, the five ministers were all well-known to be extreme Puritans or rather Independants; the three Downes, who were brothers, were afterwards at Exeter. Hawkins was sometime Rector of Felleigh, and Bartlett lecturer at Bideford.

This petition came before the Committee for Plundered Ministers on April 18, 1646, and "It was orderd yᵗ Martin Blake, Vicar of Barnstaple in ye County of Devon doe make his personall appearance before this Committee on ye 14ᵗʰ day of May next ensuing to answer to certain acts of misdemeanour whereof he is not to fail at his peril." (Add. MS., 15670, p. 130).

Tooker, who in all the persecutions of Blake, appears as the leading instigator, was in reality the tool of Charles Peard, who was a bitter opponent of the Church. Armed with this order, Tooker came down to Barnstaple and endeavoured to get further local signatures to the petition. In this he was unsuccessful. It was such a travesty of well-known facts that not a single parishioner, however much they differed from Blake in politics and religion, could be induced to sign. However fond Blake was of religious controversies, he had never interfered in the municipal government;

his one so-called political effort had been, not for the triumph of a party, but for peace. A counter petition in Blake's favour was, however, readily signed, both by Parliamentarians and Royalists, and, indeed, many of his strongest supporters and relatives had taken the Parliamentary side. Tooker, on perceiving this, kept the Committee's order to himself, and never served it on Blake, though he went about informing everybody, that if they signed the counter petition, they would get themselves into trouble for aiding and abetting a notorious delinquent, and then went to Exeter to interview some of the members of the Committee for the County of Devon, and their clerk, Nicholas Rowe, a great friend of his, with the result that he obtained a fresh summons for Blake to attend before that Committee on May 1, as he considered that matters were more likely to go in his favour before them, than if the case was heard in London.

With this new summons he returned to Barnstaple, and served the notice of it on Blake. The Mayor and Corporation were most indignant at this action of Tooker's, in taking it upon himself to prosecute the vicar without their authority, and it was resolved that the Mayor and a deputation of the Council should accompany Blake to Exeter, bearing with them the town petition in his favour, the whole thing being looked on as a piece of personal spite of Peard and Tooker against the vicar.

On the day of hearing the Committee at first sat in secret, Blake and the deputation being kept outside the door waiting and only Tooker admitted, Tooker being most anxious that the case should not be argued before the deputation, and accordingly he informed the Committee that the Mayor, John Downe, was a connection of Blake's, and therefore anxious to shield him, though they knew he was guilty. The Committee therefore decided that the case be adjourned for a week, but that they would receive then the Mayor and Corporation's petition. Blake remained in Exeter in suspense, and the Mayor and deputation returned to Barnstaple. Peard and Tooker, however, employed the interval in framing another petition and in getting a copy of Blake's letter to the Mayor of Plymouth from Philip Francis, who was a member of the Committee, and what other evidence they could. The case came on again on May 8. The members of the Committee present were Sir John Northcote, Sir John Bampfield, Philip Francis, an ex-Mayor of Plymouth, John Beare, Richard Evans, and Timothy Alsop, all of Plymouth, John Barton, John Marshall, and Joseph Hankin. Peard and Tooker, produced their petition, which was read over to Blake, though no names were divulged as

The Life of Martin Blake B.D.

subscribers to it. Blake demanded that a copy should be handed to him, that he might reply, which was refused; and after this some garbled extracts of his letters to Plymouth were read out, and Blake was called upon for his defence, which he made at some length, and he was then ordered to withdraw. The Committee were divided: **Sir John Northcote** and **Sir John Bampfield** were for acquitting him, the others suggested that the business would be best ended by Blake resigning, as then no sentence need be passed against him; and the two Sir Johns were requested to interview Blake and ask if he would resign. Blake utterly refused this suggestion, though warned that if he did not do so his whole estate, both spiritual and temporal, might be sequestrated. On the return of the two members further deliberation took place. Sir John Northcote pointed out that there was really nothing beyond what was covered by Article 3 of the Capitulations of Barnstaple, and that Blake had studiously abstained from any abuse of his position or action against Parliament, and it was ultimately decided—

(1) "That Mr Martin Blake is a delinquent.

(2) "That he be suspended from his Benefice of Barnstaple, but not sequestrated for the present."

Nicholas Rowe, the clerk, on entering the sentence in the minute book, worded it :—

The Life of Martin Blake B.D.

(1) "That Mr Martin Blake is a notorious delinquent.

(2) "That he shall be removed from the Benefice of Barnstaple and another able and orthodox Minister be placed in his roome, but sequestration of his estate be suspended because he claymeth the benefitt of the Articles of the surrender of Barnstaple to Sir Thomas ffairfax.

"Ex^d p. NI ROWE."

Blake was informed of the Committee's decision, and requested to give a bond that he would not officiate in any way, till his suspension was removed, while Peard and Tooker returned to Barnstaple with a copy of this incorrect entry, and stated that Blake had been sequestrated and endeavoured to get a petition signed to the Committee to appoint them another minister. However, the Mayor and Corporation resenting Peard and Tooker's action, sent a petition of their own requesting that Mr Hughes or Mr Hanmer be appointed to officiate till Blake should be restored. Other influences also were brought to bear among them : the famous Admiral Blake wrote to Sir Hardress Waller, then commanding the Parliamentary forces in Devon. Waller wrote to the Committee in Blake's favour, declaring that he himself had received spiritual comfort from Blake, and had observed his great zeal to God's people,

The Life of Martin Blake B.D.

and assuring them that Blake was singularly gifted and truly and powerfully godly, but in spite of this intervention, Blake's suspension was continued, though no steps were taken to supply his place.

Indeed, it would have been impossible to have got any one, for ere the vicar returned from Exeter, the plague, which in so many cases followed quickly on the footsteps of war, had broken out in Barnstaple. He came back to find many of the houses shut up, the red cross with the pious deprecation, "The Lord have mercy on us," painted on many of the doors. The richer merchants had escaped to their country farms and houses before the cordon was drawn round the town, for none of the neighbouring parishes would permit the possibly plague-infected to sojourn among them. The County Sessions at Exeter had ordered that "The Town of Barnstaple, being infected with the plague, none of the inhabitants are to be entertained in any of the neighbouring parishes. If they do they are to be bound to the Sessions, and their houses shut up."—(Harding MSS.). The registers of the Parish Church were not kept at this period, and we have no means of arriving at the mortality. The Harding MSS. give the number as 1500, but in the suburban parish of Pilton nearly a third of the population died in twelve months;

and at this juncture, when the consolations of religion would be more sought after than any other time, there was no minister of religion in the town, and the people were cast into the ground like dogs without any religious rites. Blake had been silenced and forbidden to minister in any way, and no one was willing to take his place. The vicar was anxious and desirous to perform the duties of his office and minister to the sick and dying, but dared not risk disobedience, as in the bond which had been extracted from him at Exeter, he had pledged his honour to perform no ministerial functions whatever without permission of the then authorities. He accordingly retired to his late father-in-law's house at Rumsum, Newport, from whence he addressed the following pastoral letter to his parishioners :—

" DEARE SIR,
"Though for the while I be somewhat removed from you in person, yet I am ever with you in affection and the tendernes of my compassion, beseeching Almighty God out of his infinite mercy to give a gratious issue out of this sad miserie, by forgiving our sins wch have been the cause, and by ceasing this sickness wch is the effect of his Displeasure against us ! Truely, I am not well, while it is thus ill with you : and

The Life of Martin Blake B.D.

on the contrary, I should esteem it a great accession to my own welfare, if I might be any way (through his goodnesse) instrumentall for yours. I am restrayned (yet) from being among you, as I was wont: but, they cannot so restraine my prayers: and God, I hope, will restraine that unjust violence, wch thus severs betwixt the Pastor and his Flock, and will seasonably bring us once againe together to reape the mutuall comforts of each others societie, wch is the earnest and ardent longing of my soule, as being desirous, if God will, in the free exercise of my Ministrie to run the same hazzards with your selves. In the meane season, my humble prayer is, that the Lord would lovingly sanctifie all these our afflictions to us, that in the end we may come out better than we went in; and that, God by this meanes being more glorified by us, and we more benefited by him, the Divell may be ashamed of his craft, and his instruments from henceforth ever disabled to serve him any more in this kinde! The Lord our God is worthy to be trusted: and therfore, as Job sayd, so let us resolve, Though the Lord should kill us, yet we will trust in him. The same hand that hath protected and delivered us hitherto from so many very imminent and pressing dangers, can worke as effectually for us now as ever. He is now no farther off than heretofore, from all those that

The Life of Martin Blake B.D.

call upon him in truth. God make us of this number, and we are safe however. They cannot miscarry to their hurt, into whom He puts this sweet and kindly spirit of supplication. Now, to this God and his Grace through Jesus Christ I humbly recommend you, and your whole Communitie, and in him I rest.

" Most affectionately yours to serve you,
all that I am, in all that I can,
" MARTIN BLAKE.
" ROMESOME, *Junii* 29°, 1646°.

" Salutations to all our loving frends. I name no particulars, because I would leave out none."

The murmurings in the town against the Committee that kept their minister from them in their troubles, and with no one to give their friends Christian burial, were deep. The Mayor sent another petition to the Committee for Devon, representing their sad case. The townsfolk were dying by the hundred, and no one would come near them in such an infected place, except their old vicar, who was only waiting for permission to return. The petition was rejected on the plea that it was the petition of the Mayor, a connection of Blake, and not that of the Corporation. In September Richard Ferris was elected Mayor at a meeting held in the open air at the Port Marsh, for they dared not assemble in the Guild

The Life of Martin Blake B.D.

Hall for fear of infection, and another petition was then drawn up and sent to the Committee, signed by the Mayor, Richard Ferris, the Aldermen, and the Corporation, and by the same messenger who carried the petition, the following letter was sent to Sir John Bampfield, one of the Committee who had been somewhat favourable to Blake at the hearing of the case :—

"NOBELL SER

"In these our late sufferings from the hand of God we do wth all thankfulness acknowledge the charitable care which the generalle comitey was pleased to exercise, for the reliefe of our bodyly condiction but have in the mayne season been miserably destituted of spirituall comfort for our soules by the long continued suspenstion of our paster Mr Martine Blake whose freedome to minister to us in the things of God, though we often petitioned and w^{th}all scertified what maner of man we have found him all this while ever in our greatest extremityes yet hitherto we have not obtayned at ther hands, not as we hope out of a will in them fineally to denie us but only to trye us for a while and in the meyne time to inquier into the truth of things as they have bine represented to them in a contrary way, one the one sid by us, one the other sid by his accusers : as for us we speeke what we know and testifie what

The Life of Martin Blake B.D.

we have found and if need be the whole countrey hereabout of souled well affectyd persons to the Parlyment are ready from ther owne experiance to witnesse wth us in each partickler, now if an accusatorey petion contrived in a clouse way so fair ofe as London and attested only with nine bair hands whereof one yet is disclaymed and of the other eight two only are our parishoners the rest foriners shal be thought suffictient to way downe that ampell testimony wch we have given and doe once agayne offer in his behaulfe we cannot but account it as most a great addiction unto our other infelicityes to be so far under- . . . ed bye him whom we honer and to be denied that ordanarey fauor wh is generally vouch-safed to other congerigations. Nobell S^r the man is not all togeither onknowen unto y^orselfe he onc pleaded his cause in yor presence and how fare to yor personall satisfaction not w^thstanding what was then objected and layd to his charge y^or wisdom and ingenuity coud best Judge and although this restraynt of his ministery among us be unto him a great affliction yet as he hath often sayd, the innocency of his hart doth bare him up to undergoe it wth patience never the lesse that cannot serve to recompence our lost and therefore out of con-fidence wch we have in yor worthynes we doe now make it our humble sute to you in spectiall that you would pleased so fare to appear in our behalfe at the Committee that our messingers whom we now send with our petition may be despatched to us with some comfortabell answare according to Justis and exigencie of our cause who from the hands of wicked men have all ready suffred well nie to our undoeing for our constant love unto the Parlym^t wch also when the tyme was we never yet fayled really to expresse in the efect ther of other ways and by the grace of God never shall and in the mayne tyme rest.

" Nobell S^r

" Yo^r humbell servante

" RICH^D FFERRIS *Mayore*

" J$_o$ DOWNE *Ald. :*

" JUSTINIAN WESTCOMBE.

" BARNESTAPLE, *this*
12 *Octob.* 1646."

Sir John Bampfield appears to have been willing to comply with this request, and at the next meeting of the Committee proposed that as the Corporation of Barnstaple were assured that Blake was well affected his suspension be removed; the majority, however, considered that if permission were refused the Corporation would in their necessity ask for some other minister, and it was intimated to them that if any minister except Blake were asked for the request would be immediately granted.

The Life of Martin Blake B.D.

In the meanwhile Peard and Tooker had not been idle, having failed in obtaining anything more than suspension from the County Committee, they had determined to apply to the Committee for Plundered Ministers. This Committee of the House of Commons had been originally appointed on December 31, 1642, to consider the fittest way for the relief of such good and well affected ministers as had been plundered, and likewise to consider what malignant persons have benefices herein and about this town, whose livings being sequestered these may supply their cures and receive the profits ("Commons Journal," ii., 909, Dec. 31, 1642). The powers of this body had gradually grown until it had come to be practically a board of ecclesiastical commissioners of a completely disestablished and partly disendowed English Church.

Having induced three other townsmen to join with them, they presented a petition to this Committee in which after falsely stating that Blake had been sequestrated by the County Committee, they requested that they might be appointed sequestrators to receive the profits of the living, and supply the duty till a new minister was appointed. Their petition was considered at a meeting of the Committee for Plundered Ministers on December 4, 1646, and the following resolution passed :—

The Life of Martin Blake B.D.

"Upon the Petition of diverse of the inhabitants of Barnstaple in ye County of Devon, this Committee doth appoynt Charles Peard late Mayor of Barnstaple aforesayd, William Nottell, John Tooker, John Cook and John Richards inhabitants of the sayd Town to provide for the cure of the Church of Barnstaple aforesaid; and to collect, gather, and receive the Tithes and Profits of the Vicaredge thereof sequestred from Martin Blake, and therewith satisfie such as shall officiate the cure of the sayd Church for the space of three months next ensuing."

With this order, obtained under false pretences, Peard and Tooker returned to Barnstaple, but instead of acting on it kept it a secret. The following April (1647) Blake, having gone to London on business, was advised to apply to the Committee for Plundered Ministers to get his suspension taken off. On going to their office he there discovered, to his amazement, the order that had been issued. He immediately wrote to the Mayor, Richard Ferris, who called a meeting at which a document, stating the true facts of the case, was drawn up, with a petition in Blake's favour, and signed by all the chief townsmen. Among the signatures is, curiously, to be found the name of Tooker—doubtless either because

The Life of Martin Blake B.D.

he was ashamed of himself, or dared not disclose his proceedings in a place where the true facts of the case were known. Armed with this, Blake appeared before the Committee, on April 13, when the following order was made :—

"At the Committee for Plundered Ministers,
Ap. 13, 1647.

"Upon the humble petition of the Town and Parish of Barnstaple, in the Countie of Devon, for that it is informed that Mr Blake, Minister of Barnstaple, is no Delinquent nor Sequestrable, and therefore pray that the order of the 4th December last (whereby Charles Peard, William Nottell, John Tooker, John Cook, Inhabitants of the sayd Town are appoynted to provide for the service of the cure of the sayd Church and collect the Profits of the sayd Vicarage) may be discharged ; and for that the sayd Mr Blake is not sequestred by this Committee neither doth it appear that the same is sequestred by any other Committee. It is therefore ordered that the sayd order and all proceedings in pursuance thereof be discharged and that the sayd Mr Blake doe (notwithstanding the same) officiate the cure of the sayd Church and enjoy the profits of the said Vicarage according to his Title thereunto. And the Committee of Parliament for the sayd Countie are desired to take ye sayd sequestrators accompt of the profits of the sayd Vicarage and see them payed unto the said Mr Blake so much thereof as are remayning in their hands."

The day after this order the following cross-petition was presented to the Committee :—

"To the honble Committee for Plundered Ministers.

"The Humble Peti'con of Charles Peard, late Mayor of Barnstaple, Willm Nottle, John Tooker, John Cooke, John Richards wth many others also well affected inhabitants of the said Towne sheweth that this ^{Ctee} was pleased by order 9° December last to appoint severall sequestrators (p'sons well affected) to collect and receive the tithes and profitts of the vicarage of Barnstaple sequestred from Mr Martin Blake, Delinq^t and to provide for the cure of the said Church which they have accordingly done.

"That about the 13th of this instant Aprill upon a peti'con p'cured by the said Blake from some of the Inhabitants of Barnstaple aforesaid without mentioning his being sequestred by the ^{Cotee} of Devon hath obteyned the order of this ^{Cotee} to be restored to the said vicarage wch yor peti'con^{rs} humbly conceive (the s^d Mr Blake being a delinq^t as appeares by . . .) to be ag^t the order of the House of Commons of 15° May last.

The Life of Martin Blake B.D.

"The pet[rs] humbly pray the said votes and certificates annexed remaining w[h] the Clarke of this C[otee] may be void and the order of the 13th instant Aprill suspended, and that the sequestrators formerly appointed by the order receive and collect the profitts of the said Vicarage and p'vide for the cure untill some able and well affected Minister shall be appointed to officiate as curate to us

"And your peti'con[rs] &c."

This petition, it may be said, was a forgery, and without the knowledge of Peard, Tooker, and the others, who were all 200 miles away at the time. It came before the Committee for Plundered Ministers on April 16, 1647, and it was ordered that—

"Ye sayd Mr Blake doe shew cause before this Committee on the 13th of May next wherefore the said order of the 15th of April should not be revoked as desired."

It happened that at that time several of the Council and other parishioners of Barnstaple were in London on private business, and Blake, after consultation with them, decided that it would be best to instruct a lawyer to appear on his behalf before the Committee and argue the case for him instead of appearing in person. Accordingly, no less a person than John Bradshaw, who afterwards presided at the trial of King Charles, was engaged to appear on behalf of Blake. On hearing of this, Peard and Tooker also engaged counsel to appear for them, and the case was argued at length before the Committee on May 13.

Peard's counsel relied for his case on the following documents :—

(i.) " The entry in the books of the Committee of Devon of the Resolution of May 8, 1646. An attested copy of this was put in, also the following :—

(ii.) " We whose names are hereunder written doe certify that the attested copy is a true copy of the vote passed against Mr Martin Blake att the standing Committee of which we were members at wch time he had a full hearing of what he could say for himselfe and upon a full debate thereof the result was on very good grounds as above specified.

"TYMO. ALSOP, PHILIP FRANCIS.
" 9th 9^{ber} 1646."

(iii.) "This serveth to testifie that I Philip Francis being Mayor of Plimmouth in the yeare 1643 rec^d 2 letters att severall tymes from Mr Martin Blake Vicar of Barnstaple one to me and the Magistrates by the hands of one Langford of Barnestaple a desparate enemy to ye state, and another by a messenger sent by the said Blake both wch letters importing his uttmost endeavours to p'suade us to yeeld up the said Towne unto the enemy by way of subtle arguments alleadging the Justice of the enemies proceedings as will clearly appeare by the said letters now in my custody att **Plimmouth** and were sent to **Plimmouth** immediately on the surrender of **Barnestaple**. In testimonie whereof I have here unto subscribed my name the day and **yeare** above written.

" PHILLIP FRANCIS."

(iv.) " To the Honble Committee for Plundered Ministers :—

" The humble Peti'con of Charles Peard late Mayor of Barnestaple, Willm Nottle, John Tooker, Jo^{ph.} Cooke, J_o Richards wth many others also well affected inhabitants of the said Towne.

" Sheweth that Mr Martyn Blake Vicar of Barnestaple aforesaid for his holding correspondencie wth the forces raised ^{agst} the Parliament and other his disaffeccon to the state was sequestred in May last by the Committee for Devon as appeareth by the papers annexed.

" Your peti'coners most humbly pray your hono^{rs} will please to appoint the late Mayor **Mr** Peard and some others of the hon^{ble} Committees pet[rs] to provide for the service of the cure until this hon[ble] Committee shall please to appoint some able and orthodox Divine to officiate amongst them.

"And your peti'con[rs] in duty bound
shall ever pray

"Charles Peard   "Jo: Tooker
"William Nottle   "Athonie Moore
"Jo: Lake   "John Richards
"John Cooke."

In reply Bradshaw, as Blake's counsel, put forward the following reasons why the order of April 13, should stand and be confirmed :—

(i.) "The Petition of April 16 was put forward without the knowledge of the men whose names were prefixed, that Tooker the original prime mover had stated he had withdrawn, that Mr Nottell another alledged signature would declare that his name was inserted without his consent.

(ii.) "That while the petitioners pretended there were many others consenting with them, there were only two or three who had become Anabaptists and Brownists.

(iii.) "Peard had made no provision for any services while Blake had been suspended.

(iv.) "That concerning the statement that Blake had been voted a delinquent, he would

The Life of Martin Blake B.D.

put in a certificate to the contrary from the Corporation of Barnstaple. Also two members of the House of Commons Sir John Northcote and Sir John Bampfield who had been present at the meeting of the Committee for Devon had been satisfied that Blake had cleared himself.

(v.) "That of the original petitioners two only were Inhabitants of the Town of Barnstaple.

(vi.) "That the entry as certified by the petitioners was different from what was passed at the Committee and even the entry did not shew that Blake had been sequestrated but only that he had been suspended."

The only reply to Bradshaw's arguments that is interesting to notice is that to No. iii., in which it is stated that provision for the services at the Parish Church had been made, as Mr Hanmer lectured every week there; to which it was answered that it was true that Hanmer came in weekly, having a parsonage close to Barnstaple, but it was on Wednesdays—on Sundays there was no service at all; if the parishioners came they would find only an empty pulpit, and that besides, Hanmer came in not as one hired or to receive any maintenance out of the profits of the vicarage, but freely out of love and affection for Blake, and that he only preached, but refused to administer the sacraments and other

THE PARISH CHURCH, BARNSTAPLE, 1647

From the Blake Monument

The Life of Martin Blake B.D.

duties belonging to the minister, as Blake was the only lawful minister to do so.

The proceedings before the Committee appear to have been protracted and frequently adjourned. From such reports of the proceedings of the Committee as survive, beyond Blake's own private memorandums of the case, I find an entry dated May 17, 1647, which states:—

" It is ordered that the cause concerninge Mr Blake Vicar of Barnstaple in the County of Devon be deferred till to-morrow the first business and the Clerk is to bring the former proceedings depending against him before this Committee." (Add. MS. B. M. 15671, p. 21.)

Again, on June 22, 1647, there is an entry:—

" Whereas it appeareth by order of the Committee of Parliament for the Countie of Devon of the 8th of May 1646 that Mr Blake is sequestered by them from the Church of Barnstaple in the said Countie for his delinquence it is ordered that in case the said Mr Blake will make his address to this committee against the said sequestration that then the said order shall be taken into consideration and that Mr Charles Vaughan member of the House of Commons shall be heard therein." (Add. MSS. 15671.)

There appear to have been two parties on the Committee—one desirous that justice should be

The Life of Martin Blake B.D.

done, if their rules were observed, the other ready to condemn anyone who was even a suspected opponent. It is, perhaps, unnecessary to report the case at any further length, though Blake has left very full and lengthy reports of the statements of the witnesses and arguments of the counsel before the Committee; but it appears that after a long consideration of the case the Committee unanimously decided that their order of April 13, by which Blake was restored to his living and allowed to enjoy the profits of the vicarage for the future, and such arrears as were in hands of the committee for the county should stand, and that all further proceedings against him should be laid aside, and no further prosecution made against him without notice first given to Blake and his counsel.

The only names I have been able to recover of the Barnstaple men then staying in London who supported Blake in this appeal to the Committee are: Richard Harris, gent., Joseph Bonivant, merchant, and William Walters, merchant.

The case having been decided in his favour, Blake shortly after returned to Barnstaple, but though pressed to officiate the following Sunday, he refused to do so, on account of his bond, till he had permission also from the Committee of Devon. The Mayor, Mr Richard Harris, merchant (a different person from Mr Richard

The Life of Martin Blake B.D.

Harris who supported Blake in London), immediately wrote to the Committee for Plundered Ministers, asking for an official notice of their decision, and also for a notice to the Committee of Devon, which he shortly after received, signed by many of the members of the Committee of Parliament. He immediately forwarded it to Exeter by the hands of the senior alderman, Mr Alexander Horwood, in olden days an opponent of Blake's, but now after experience a strong supporter, who presented it in person to the Committee, as he had been warned that there was a danger of their clerk, N. Rowe, suppressing it. This letter stated that the Committee for Plundered Ministers on frequent examination of Blake's case found it just, and ordered that all prosecutions against him should cease, and that they had admitted him to the " free enjoyment of his place in the Vicaridge at Barnstaple wishing them for their parts to doe the like."

The Committee for Devon on perusal of this letter replied that they were satisfied, and told Mr Horwood that Mr Blake might resume his place at his pleasure, and they had now no more to say against him.

Mr Horwood then requested that for the better satisfaction of the Corporation and Blake that they would put what they had said in writing. The Committee assented to this, and ordered their

The Life of Martin Blake B.D.

clerk, Nicholas Rowe, to write out their decision, that they might sign it. Rowe, however, to prevent there being a written record of Blake's suspension having been removed, remarked that surely Blake was not too good to rest on the gentlemen's word without their writing, and that by writing they would lower themselves. On this the Committee refrained from writing, but simply renewed their declaration by word of mouth.

Sir John Northcote, one of the members who was present, seems to have been disgusted with this underhand proceeding, and himself wrote a letter to the Mayor of Barnstaple embodying the Committee's decision, and urging the Mayor to by all means persuade Blake to resume his place in Barnstaple without any further scruple, seeing that both the Committees (the one at Westminster, and the other in Devon) had so unanimously agreed on his behalf. This letter Sir John signed and handed to Mr Horwood, requesting him to deliver it personally to the Mayor of Barnstaple. And so the first persecution ended the beginning of January 1647-48.

CHAPTER V

RETURN TO BARNSTAPLE AND THE SECOND PERSECUTION

1648-1659

Blake returns to Barnstaple—Letter from the Corporation to him—Recommences his ministry—Richard Ferris—His efforts for a settlement of religious differences — Blake's agreement with Hanmer—Hanmer appointed Lecturer—Blake's second marriage—The Presbyterian System—The Associations—Death of Dr Hakewill and Joan Blake—Cromwell's order of 1655—Tooker takes advantage of it—Mather presented to the Living —The Conference at Mr Medford's—Blake goes to London—His interview with Cromwell—Sir John Copplestone's attack on the Vicarage—Fear of smallpox routs the attack—Blake carried off by troopers to Exeter—Cary breaks into the vicarage —Blake before the County Committee—Retires to Barnstaple — Cromwell's death—The Long Parliament reassembles—Restores Blake to his living.

IT was with great hesitation that Blake resumed his pastoral work at Barnstaple. The Sunday following Mr Horwood's return from Exeter there was no service at the Parish Church,

The Life of Martin Blake B.D.

Blake refusing to officiate because he had nothing in writing from the Committee as yet, permitting him to do so. The following week the Mayor summoned a meeting of the Corporation, at which a letter was drawn up and signed by all present, requesting Blake to resume his pulpit, and exercise his ministerial functions among them once more. This letter was as follows :—

" To our loving Pastor, Mr Martin Blake; present these

" SIR,
" We have lately received a letter from Sir John Norcote, and by it doe understand, y^t the Gent: of the Committee of this County doe willingly give way that you should preach among us as heretofore in your own Charge. And Sir John Northcote himself in the same letter doth very earnestly persuade that you would accordingly apply yourself to the work, wch hee doth assure us shall bee without any danger or prejudice to you. And therefore, wee taking into consideration our long want of you, & the great disappoyntment of the Congregation, that will bee this next Lords-day if you preach not; wee thought good in our own names, and in the names of the rest of the Parish, to request you by these lines to enter into that employment to morrow

next. And so not doubting your love in answering of our desire, wee rest

"Your loving Friends,

RICHARD HARRIS *Mayor.*
RICHARD FERRIS *Alderman.*
ALEXANDER HORWOOD, *Alderman.*

"JOHN TOOKER. WILLIAM PALMER.
"JOHN COOK. JUSTINIAN WESTCOMB.
"JOHN SWEET. THOMAS HORWOOD.
"JOHN ROSIER. JOHN DOWN.
"JOHN SEAGAR. WALTER TUCKER.
"WILLIAM WOOD. RICHARD HARRIS.
THOMAS DENNIS.
JOHN HORWOOD.
JOSEPH BONEVANT.
ROᵀ LANE.

"*Jan. 22, 1647.*"

It will be noticed that this letter is signed by John Tooker and John Cook, two of the petitioners against Blake, as well as by the large majority who had always supported. It appears either that Tooker found it too unpopular a proceeding, when residing in Barnstaple, to oppose Blake, or that, Peard being absent, he had no incentive to do so any longer.

On the receipt of this letter, Blake says: "I

could no longer forbear to gratifie them in their desires on this letter of request so affectionately comming from my parishioners."

So far, I have followed the sequence of events in the first persecution of Blake, to his resumption of his ministerial duties in January 1647-8, without referring to other incidents; but there is one that preceded his resettlement, to which I must now refer, as there is no doubt it largely influenced the Corporation in so unanimously supporting him at the end of his first persecution,—and it, also, a point on which Walker, in his account of Blake, is not only inaccurate, but also misleading.

Richard Ferris, who had been largely instrumental in securing Blake's acquittal by the Committee for Plundered Ministers and his return to Barnstaple, was one of the large class who, sympathising with the Parliament at first and freely contributing to their cause, had disapproved of the lengths to which they had gone. Elected in 1640 as member for Barnstaple in the Long Parliament, he had been "disabled"—that is, voted out of the house—because he was not ready to go far enough; but in Barnstaple he was still a leading personality, and looked up to by all as a true friend of liberty—just, upright, and deeply religious—and he had determined that if the vicar returned, there should be no renewal of the conflicts between vicar and lecturer, which had given birth to feuds and bitter feelings in the past. A lecturer appointed by the Council, now that there was no Episcopal license needed, was all too likely to come into conflict with the vicar, and in such a case, the lecturer was certain to be the one who would be supported by the County Committee; and there was a possibility of Benjamin Cox, the old lecturer, who was still in the town, being appointed. The only hope of a permanent peace was, that there should be a lecturer with whom both the nonconformists and Blake could agree, and the one person who seemed to him to combine these qualifications, was Jonathan Hanmer, the vicar of Instow, and then acting as minister of Bishop's Tawton—a moderate Presbyterian possessing the confidence of the nonconformists, yet a personal friend and connection of Blake's. Ferris had broached the subject to Blake, who was only too willing to agree. The doubt was, whether Hanmer would put himself to the inconvenience of undertaking a post to which only a small stipend would be attached, for Hanmer was known to hold strong opinions on lecturers' salaries. The obstacles, however, were overcome, and it was also arranged that there should be a formal agreement before the Corporation, between Blake and Hanmer. Accordingly, on the 28th of October 1647, at the Guildhall, the

The Life of Martin Blake B.D.

following document was drawn up and signed and sealed by Blake :—

"I doe willingly yield to admit of Mr Jonathan Hanmer to preach every Lords day in the afternoone and one day in the week besides as is desired by the godly people of this towne.

"Ffarther I doe assure the godly people of this place that whensoever I shall be resetled in my Pastorall chardge here in Barnᵗᵗ: they from thence foarth shall not lay under any pʳjudice (as much as in me shalbe) by reason of wᶜʰ many conseave and may farther speak ᵃᵍˢᵗ them in reference to any thinge they have done ᵃᵍˢᵗ me neither at tyme shall I hinder or oppose them in makinge use of theire Christian liberty in such things as wherein through tendernesse of conscience and difference of judgmᵗ: they may vary both from myselfe and others in matters not essentiall to religion and godlines but endeavᵈ the just pʼservation of it.

"Witness my hand and seale, the 28th day of October 1647.

"MARTIN BLAKE.

"Witness
    "John Cook."

It was doubtless owing to this agreement that the return of the vicar, instead of causing fresh controversies, was the signal for an ecclesiastical peace. Each party felt they had been considered : the Catholic-minded could attend the vicar's ministrations in the morning, the Puritan-minded the Rev. Jonathan Hanmer's in the afternoon.

Richard Ferris lived little more than a year to see the result of his labours for religious peace. He died in 1649. His monument, immediately facing the south door, shows a full-length recumbent figure in the costume of the period and mayoralty robes, holding a palm branch with groups of emblems and mottoes. The inscription speaks of him as a frequenter of God's house, and one who held the scales of justice even. By his will, dated June 19, 1646, proved January 3, 1649, he left to Mr Martin Blake, Vicar of Barnstaple, £10 in money. The ecclesiastical peace is also reflected in municipal affairs. During the civil war the townsmen found they had only exchanged King Log for King Stork, and that the exactions of military forces and troops at free quarters were ten thousand times worse than ship-money ; and political differences were lost in a common feeling for the preservation of their municipal rights and liberties, with which Cromwell was dealing more arbitrarily than King Charles ever had ; so we see that though the mayors of 1648 and 1649 were Nottel and Cooke, two of Blake's strongest opponents, yet those of 1650 and 1651

The Life of Martin Blake B.D.

were Thomas Dennis, a leading royalist, and Thomas Matthew, Blake's nephew.

Shortly after Blake's resettlement in his vicarage, the vicar married a second time, and again a Barnstaple lady. She was Mary, daughter of Richard Harris, and widow of George Musgrave of Nettlecombe and North Petherton. The marriage took place at St Mary Magdalene's, Taunton, on March 10, 1649. This date probably means 1648-9, as the year begins January 1 almost all through the register, but is uncertain, as the entries at this period are very fragmentary.

The second Mrs Blake brought with her to Barnstaple her sons Richard, George, John, and Thomas Musgrave, and her daughter Hanna. Her descendants were afterwards well known in Barnstaple and Exeter, among them being Doctor Richard Musgrave of Barnstaple and the two Doctors William Musgrave of Exeter, father and son. Of Martin Blake's family by his first wife, only two were now surviving, a son, John, baptized June 26, 1631, and a daughter, Joan, baptized May 17, 1635. His second son, Nicholas, to whose memory the remarkable monument in St Peter's Church was erected, and to which I shall refer later, died during the troubles, on February 12, 1644. The others all died in childhood.

Of the period from Blake's first restoration to

The Life of Martin Blake B.D.

1656 there is very little to relate. As in municipal, so in ecclesiastical affairs, things went on much as before the war, save for the observance of altered rules and regulations for public worship. Although Presbyterianism was legally established, it was practically never carried into effect, for English Puritanism was never genuinely Presbyterian ; the inquisitional system associated with it was odious to the English people, as Baxter writes : " Though presbytery took root in Scotland yet it was but a stranger here. Most that ever I could meet with were against the *jus divinum* of lay elders and for the moderate primitive Episcopacy and for a parochial extent of ordinary churches and for an accommodation of all parties in order to concord."

There is no record of the establishment of any classical system in Devonshire, though it is probable there was such a thing. A voluntary association of the ministers in the county of Devon was formed in 1655, and its first meeting was held at Exeter, October 18, 1655 (the minutes of its meetings have been published in " Transactions of the Devonshire Association,' vol. xxix., p. 279-88). The seven divisions of this association probably represent the seven classes into which the county was divided by the classical system ; but Barnstaple seems to have stood outside the fourth division, in which it

The Life of Martin Blake B.D.

would have been placed, though Jonathan Hanmer, as minister of Bishop's Tawton, was a member. But the classical presbyteries were but scantily accepted by the county at large, and with great reluctance ; only in Essex and London does this system appear to have really come into operation.

Blake, indeed, was deprived of the use of the Prayer Book, but, like many other clergy, he knew its prayers so well that, under the guise of extempore prayer, its system was practically followed, to the satisfaction of his congregation, and the years from 1647 to 1655 were, as far as Barnstaple was concerned, years of religious peace. But during them, Blake lost, by death, many of his strongest and most faithful supporters. Richard Ferris died, as I have already mentioned, in 1649, and in the same year Blake lost his brother-in-law, the learned and devout George Hakewill, D.D. Ejected from his Rectorship of Exeter College, Oxford, he had retired to his rectory of Heanton, where he died, April 2, and was buried April 5, 1649, his two sons, John and George Hakewill, having pre-deceased him.

Amongst others were John Ferris, Blake's niece Mrs Matthews, William Palmer and his sister Mrs Collabeare, Alexander and Thomas Horwood, Justinian Westcombe, Walter Tucker,

The Life of Martin Blake B.D.

John Rosier, and Robert Lane the Town-Clerk. But perhaps the one that Blake felt most was that of his only daughter, Joan, in her seventeenth year, in September 1651. Of the eight children born to him by his first marriage, only his youngest son John now survived.

No other trouble arose for Blake till the year 1656, when Cromwell's order of November 24, 1655, gave a new opportunity to Tooker. This order was :—

"His Highness by the advice of his Council doth publish declare and order that no person or persons do from and after the 1st day of January 1655 (-6) keep in their houses or families as chaplains or schoolmasters for the education of their children any sequestered or ejected minister, fellow of a college or schoolmaster, nor permit any of their children to be taught by such in pain of being proceeded against in such sort as the said orders do direct in such cases. And that no person who hath been sequestered or ejected out of any benefice college or school for delinquency or scandal shall from and after the said first day of January keep any school public or private nor any person who after that time shall be ejected for the causes aforesaid shall preach in any public place or at any private meeting of other persons besides his own family

nor shall administer baptism or the Lord's
supper or marry any persons, or use the Book
of Common Prayer or the terms therein contained
upon pain that every person so offending shall
be proceeded against as by the said orders is
provided."

Blake, quite unaware that he could possibly be
in any way affected by this ordinance, went on
with his ministerial work as usual; but January
1 having passed, two of Blake's old enemies,
John Tooker and John Cook, took advantage of
it, and forwarded an accusation to the Protector,
stating that Martin Blake, Vicar of Barnstaple,
having been a delinquent and sequestrated, had
disobeyed the ordinance by preaching after
January 1, and requesting that Cromwell would at
once fill up the now vacant living of Barnstaple.

The Protector, ever ready to exercise patronage,
immediately presented Nathaniel Mather, an Independant, who had been intruded at Harberton
on the deprivation for delinquency of John Carew.

Blake, on hearing of this, was astounded.
Meeting Tooker and Cook, he asked them how
they could have behaved in this manner. They
replied it was because Blake had broken his
promise made with Mr Hanmer, of suffering
him to preach at Barnstaple every Lord's day.
Blake immediately replied that he had never

The Life of Martin Blake B.D.

denied him, as Mr Hanmer would prove, if they would meet him at Mr Medford's, the Mayor. Accordingly, on January 28, a meeting was held at the house of Richard Medford, when many of both Blake's friends and opponents were present, including John Horwood and Richard Harris the Aldermen, John Downe, Joseph Bonivant, Joseph Delbridge, William Wescombe, John Palmer, Thomas Cox, Richard Hooper, Nicholas Hooper, William Walters, and John Cooke, as well as Blake and Hanmer.

Blake then, in the presence of all, asked Hanmer if it was true that he had ever denied him the liberty of preaching at Barnstaple every Lord's day. Hanmer replied that Blake was not guilty of ever denying him that liberty, but on the contrary, Blake had often asked him to come and preach, as the people expected him. But he, Hanmer, had often refused himself, adding that he considered it a most irrational thing to imagine that he could come every Sunday from Instow, where he had some relation, and from whence he had some reasonable subsistence, unless the town of Barnstaple made provision for his subsistence there. The reason, he said, of his not coming, was because the Barnstaple people did not raise a convenient maintenance for him, and not from any obstruction from his good friend Mr Martin Blake.

The Life of Martin Blake B.D.

It would seem from this that Hanmer had left Bishop's Tawton and returned to Instow, and it appears from the *Liber Institutiorum*, that John Pugsley had been presented to Bishop's Tawton on June 7, 1651, by the Lord Commissioners of the Great Seal.

Blake having satisfied his fellow-townsmen of his straightforwardness and observance of his word, determined to go at once to London, ask for an audience from Cromwell, and lay the true state of the case before him.

On arriving in London, accompanied by his son, John Blake, he went first to see his brother, Nicholas Blake, who was then residing there, who recommended that he should take counsel's opinion, as to his legal position, consequent on his acquittal by the Committee for Plundered Ministers, in 1647, and that he should consult on this, a Mr Phelps, an able lawyer. The questions submitted to Mr Phelps were :—

"(i.) What ground is there for the authority of the Committee for Plundered Ministers?

"(ii.) Whether a statute or only a transitory note?

"(iii.) If a vote, whether confirmed by Parlia- or not?"

I have not been able to obtain Phelp's opinion; but, armed with it, Blake presented himself before

138

The Life of Martin Blake B.D.

the Protector, on February 27, 1656-7. Of what occurred at this audience there is no record, but it appears that Cromwell told Blake that he was at liberty to appeal to the Law Courts on the point, as to whether Blake was legally in possession of the Vicarage of Barnstaple by the decision of the Committee for Plundered Ministers, of May 15, 1647, and that, if successful in his appeal, he could retain possession of his living.

Mr Phelps seems to have prepared a mass of evidence to lay before the Courts on this subject, and it is from his notes that I have been able to give such a full account of all the proceedings in Blake's first persecution, most of the original records of the various committees having been lost. The preparation of Blake's case seems to have taken some time. By the ejection of the Rump on April 20, 1653, the Committee for Plundered Ministers had ceased to exist, and their powers had passed to the Trustees for the Maintenance of Ministers by the Act of September 2, 1654 (Scobell, ii., 353). Another difficulty was that, owing to the malice of Nicholas Rowe, there was no entry in the books of the Committee for the county of Devon, and Mr Alexander Horwood, who had been the bearer of the verbal decision, was dead ; and Blake was advised to return to Barnstaple, take possession again, if possible, of the vicarage house, and get evidence of the letter of Sir John Northcote conveying the tidings of his acquittal.

It was in September 1657 that Blake got back to Barnstaple. He found Mather in possession of the Parish Church, his ministrations only attended by a scanty few of the Independant way of thinking ; for between the Presbyterians and Independants there was almost a deeper gulf than between Presbyterians and the Church people. Blake found that his wife had removed from the vicarage, to his house at Rumsum, but that the vicarage was still unoccupied, and stood open with no one there to forbid his entrance. Accordingly, he went there with a servant, and formally took possession, finding nothing but the bare walls, windows, and doors. His next step was to get some one to live in it as caretaker for him, and for this purpose, engaged a Mrs Hurlston with her family.

Blake's proceedings had not, however, been unnoticed by Mather and his friends, and they had written several times to Sir John Copplestone, who had been chosen Recorder of Barnstaple in February 1655-6, being then also Sheriff of Devon, and on October 15, 1657, Sir John arrived at Barnstaple with a troop of horse, and gave out that he had come to turn Blake out, having an order from His Highness the Lord

Protector to do so. Blake, on hearing this, sent Sir John a message by his son, John Blake, to acquaint him with what the vicar called the justice of his cause, and his intention to abide by the sentence of the law to which he had appealed, and that he had His Highness' permission so to do, and which he offered to prove by many witnesses. Sir John Copplestone only laughed at this notice, on which Blake sent him a second notice in writing as follows :—

" SIR,

" I have the just and lawfull possession of my Vicaridge house in Barn, and so keep it in my own right. If my opposers think I have done them herein any wrong the courts of justice are open there they may implead mee for it, and there (by the grace of God) I shall answer them. To the law I appeal and to that I have received His Highness' consent ; and I hope my opposers will not either refuse the one or deny the other, by using violence, where a legal way will doe it better.

" MARTIN BLAKE.

" *October* 16, 1657."

Sir John Copplestone took no more notice of the letter than of the message. His troop of horse galloped up and down the streets in the evening, to frighten any who thought of actively supporting the vicar, and the next morning, some of the soldiers with some of Mather's supporters went to the outer door of the vicarage, which led from the street into the little front garden. Here they found many of the inhabitants. John Blake and John Musgrave, tried to persuade them not to use force, pleading Blake's immunity as a free-born Englishman, from, being forcibly disseised of his freehold without due process in law.

However, the soldiers with a sledge hammer broke in the wicket of the outer door and came to the inner door in the porch leading into the hall, this they found strongly barricaded—so with their sledge-hammers they forced out the iron bars of one of the windows, and one of the soldiers creeping through, went to the main door, pulled down the barricades, and admitted the rest, who rushed from one room of the house to another looking for Blake, but found instead in an upstair room one of Mrs Hurlston's children in bed ill with small-pox, which sight so frightened them that they quickly retreated, and went to relate the story of their valiant deed to Sir John Copplestone, who bid them desist, and a bit afraid of the infection himself withdrew with his troop.

He left behind, however, his corporal, Daniel

The Life of Martin Blake B.D.

Cary, with instructions to break open the house again when Blake was there, arrest him, and bring him to Exeter. This Daniel Cary seems to have been a well-known character in Barnstaple: there are one or two notices of him in the diary of Richard Wood, nephew of Richard Ferris. He speaks of him in 1658 as a turbulent seditious fellow, whom the town would not admit when he was appointed Receiver by the Mayor.

A few days after the assault on the vicarage, Sir John Copplestone sent a company of troopers to surround Blake's house at Rumsum at daybreak and arrest him. They entered the house with their swords and pistols, greatly frightening Mrs Blake, demanding the vicar. Blake came down at once and asked what they wanted; they replied they had a warrant from Sir John Copplestone to bring him before Sir John at his house near Exeter. The vicar asked the reason; their leader replied he knew nothing about reason, but had got the warrant, and, forthwith seizing on the vicar's person, dragged him from the house, and set him on one of the trooper's horses, and hurried him off to Exeter in the midst of a bitter storm. On being brought before Sir John, Blake demanded what authority he had for thus coarsely handling him. Sir John answered, no more authority than his own discretion, and for purposes best known to himself, but now he had him there, he did not mean to let him go till the Commissioners at their next meeting, which was six weeks hence, had spoken with him. He, however, subsequently released Blake on his parole not to leave the city of Exeter or ten miles about it, provided those ten miles were not in Barnstaple direction, though Blake expostulated with him on his use of arbitrary power.

While Blake was a prisoner at Exeter, Cary again broke into the vicarage at Barnstaple, and forcibly ejected all the residents in it, who were all females. The women resisted as far as they could, but were forcibly carried out of the house. The poor sick child just recovering from small-pox, whom they took out of her bed screaming piteously " Cary will kill me! Cary will kill me!" and was so frightened that for weeks after it was thought she would never recover her senses.

To return to Blake, the six weeks having expired, the Commissioners met at the New Inn, at Exeter, the Chair being taken by Major Black-more, who summoned Blake to appear before them. On his coming in, the Chairman demanded what he meant by his stubborn contempt of His Highness the Lord Protector, in not relinquishing his claim to the vicarage of Barnstaple, and not suffering Mr Mather to possess it quietly, as His Highness had ordered.

But Blake was not to be brow-beaten : he replied he had His Highness' permission to defend his right at law, and his intention was to do so.

"All that you say," quoth the Chairman, "is impertinent, and I must tell you that whatever his Highness said to you, he very lately said the contrary to me. Yes, he said he would remove you pretty quick from Barnstaple if there was any power in him."

"Alas, Sir," answered Blake, "His Highness need not engage his power to remove me, whom he can easily blow off with his least breath, but I believe his Highness is more conscious to his own concessions than to deal with me as you report, and as for the impertinence which you impute to me, I hope I have not spent my time and study so ill as not to know how to speak pertinently in so plain a cause, which I so thoroughly understand, and I desire that you will not gainsay me in what he allows."

"Well, well," said Major Blackmore "His Highness will not allow you to wage law in this business, and, to make matters short, here is a paper to which if you will subscribe, so ; if not, we know what course to take with you."

Blake asked to see the paper, which was handed him ; it was as follows :—

The Life of Martin Blake B.D.

"I Martin Blake clerk do hereby submit to and acquiesce in his Highness the Lord Protector's determination and pleasure concerning my not being in Barnstaple as Vicar there. And I doe further freely promise that I will not for the future make any claim to the said vicaridge by any legall proceedings; but do wholy relinquish all titles, clayme or demands to be made by me or any on my behalf to the same.

"(Copia vera.)   John Symth
"Regr."

Blake read the paper over slowly, suppressing all signs of the indignation that was inwardly agitating him, and answered, "I am a free born Englishman and therefore neither may nor will betray my liberty by subscribing such a paper or by promising any thing that way tending, even by word of mouth, especially as I have his Highness' good leave before I left London to bring my cause to a trial at Law as my counsel shall advise me."

Blake's answer was no more satisfactory to the Committee than their paper was to him. Major Blackmore replied : " Master Blake, Master Blake, there will be longer imprisonments and perchance harder usage."

Others tried fair speeches to persuade Blake to sign, but all in vain. " No," he said, " I have

been already greatly prejudiced by false preten-
sions of having been sequestrated, which you
know is the only ground of my trouble, and,
however inclinable I am to any reasonable motion
that might tend to peace, let me see you act fair
first, let me be set right, let me see it recorded in
your books that I was not sequestrated, and
restore me my bond not to preach without your
consent, before I will declare myself any further
in this business. Let me see that done, and then
I will do anything that is just."

"You say you will do any thing that is just,'
another Commissioner replied; "but you do not
say you will do what we ask."

"If it be just," answered Blake, "you have
my promise; but if it be not just, you have no
reason to expect it, and I as little to promise
it."

"But," said Major Blackmore, "that which
you expect from us for your satisfaction is not
in our power to accomplish, but in the power
only of his Highness the Lord Protector."

"It is in your power, if you please, to signify
the reasonableness of my desire, and then I
believe upon your letter, His Highness will
order the clearing of me in your books," Blake
answered.

The Commissioners by this time had cooled
down, and undertook to write to the Protector

that Blake had not been sequestrated by the Committee of the County, and did so, on which Blake undertook to wait an answer, and meanwhile to forbear from commencing of his law suit, on which he was dismissed to return home, having got, however, the bond, which, as he said, had been so wickedly abstracted from him, and thereby secured what he valued most, liberty to preach once more, which they had also given, provided that, in his sermons, he said nothing that might reflect in anyway on his troubles.

Blake awaited in patience an answer to the Commissioners' letter, but none came, for Sir John Copplestone had taken care that no consideration should be given to it; but instead, he received a letter from Sir John, forbidding him to preach, under various penalties, within four miles of Barnstaple, which was practically forbidding him to preach at all, for Blake was far too ill and infirm from the ill-usage he had received when carried off to Exeter, to go far from his house. And later, either to silence him altogether or prevent him renewing the prosecution of his law suit, an order was procured to convey him to the Scilly Isles, there to remain a prisoner, as Blake says, "for I know not what, and at the pleasure of I know not whom;" but, to quote Blake's closing words in speaking of this persecution, "Mine eyes are unto God and I pray with that good old father : '*Miserere mei Domine sic ut vis !*'"

However, Blake's troubles were drawing to a close. On September 3 following, Cromwell died, and from his house at Rumsum, Blake heard the salvoes of the town artillery as the trumpeters proclaimed the Lord Richard, and though his old enemy, Sir John Copplestone, was back in Barnstaple, feasting the Corporation with venison and being feasted by them at a banquet of sweetmeats and wine, Lord Richard and his Parliament quickly passed away. In May 1659 the remnant of the Long Parliament returned to their house, and re-established the old Committee for Plundered Ministers, whose main idea seems to have been to discredit the whole administration of the Trustees for Maintenance and Cromwell. Sir John Northcote, the member for Devon, who had been instrumental in securing Blake's acquittal at his first persecution, had shortly after that been "secluded," and had afterwards been imprisoned, but on February 21, 1659-60, it was ordered by the restored Parliament that he, with Sir William Courtenay, Sir Richard Temple, and Sir C. Bampfield, be discharged of their imprisonment. And on February 27 he was back in the house, and two days later, placed on the Committee for settling matters concerning religion, and he was desirous

The Life of Martin Blake B.D.

that his action in resettling Blake in Barnstaple, in 1647, should be upheld.

Blake's case indeed had already been brought before Parliament by his friends, on Tuesday, February 7. " It was ordered that the Committee for Plundered Ministers are hereby empowered and required to send for the Minister of Barnstaple, in the County of Devon, and examine him. And on Friday, March 16, 1659-60, it was ordered that Mr Martyn Blague (*sic*) be and is hereby restored to his living at Barnstaple, in the County of Devon ; and it is referred to the Lords Commissioners for custody of the Great Seal, and the Master of the Rolls, or any two of them, to see this order executed, and that the said Martyn Blague be put in possession of the said living accordingly " (" Journal, H. C.," vii., p. 880).

Friday, March 16, the day on which the above order was passed, was the last day the house sat ; so we may say their last act was to restore Martin Blake to the living from which he had been so falsely and cruelly ejected.

CHAPTER VI

THE VICAR'S LAST YEARS AND DEATH

1660-1673

Blake's final return to Barnstaple—His restoration
differs from others — Mather withdraws — Blake
reads declaration of Breda—Blake's old curate
becomes Archdeacon — Visitation at Barnstaple
and Blake's sermon—Blake's efforts for comprehension — Position of the Puritans — Act of
Uniformity—Hanmer ejected—Blake's efforts to
help him — Letter of Bishop Ward — Blake's
declining years—Begins to write his memoirs—
His last curate—Blake's death—His will—Blake's
descendants—The Blake monument—Valedictory.

BLAKE appears to have returned to Barnstaple some date between February 21 and
March 4, 1559-60—that is, immediately after his
examination by the Committee for Plundered
Ministers, and before his re-instatement by the
Long Parliament. His restoration to his living is
remarkable in that it differs from all other cases.
The bulk of his sequestrated brethren simply
regained their positions as a consequence of the
restoration of the King. Blake's was on its merits;
it preceded the restoration instead of following it.

The Life of Martin Blake B.D.

On the news arriving of Parliament's decision, Blake at once resumed his ministrations, for Mather had quietly withdrawn, recognising the hopelessness of his position, for as an Independant he knew he was less acceptable to the Presbyterian party than a Churchman, and so he had already been looking out for a new post. On March 29 I find a Colonel John Clerke writing to the Lord General Montague on the Swiftsure, recommending Mather for a minister's place. " He is an able, godly man, but destitute by reason of an Act of Parliament which restored one Blake, formerly cast out for delinquency, to his place at Barnstaple. Supposes Mather's judgment inclines to the Independant way, but presumes his lordship will not think him the less qualified for that, but does not know a more learned, able, and well-qualified person " (Cal., " State Papers," papers connected with the Navy). This application does not appear to have been successful, as Mather went to Holland, where he became pastor of the English congregation at Rotterdam.

In the Convention Parliament, which assembled on April 25, 1660, Barnstaple was represented by John Rolle and Nicholas Dennis. The counterpart of the indentures, dated April 7, 1660, declaring their return as Burgesses in Parliament is still preserved, while the knights of the shire were Sir John Northcote, Blake's old

The Life of Martin Blake B.D.

friend, and the Lord General Monk. On May 5, a copy of the Declaration of Breda, which promised a liberty to tender consciences, and that no man should be disquieted or called in question for differences of opinion in matters of religion which did not disturb the peace of the kingdom, was read by Blake from his pulpit, having been sent down to Barnstaple by Nicholas Dennis, and a week later, May 12, King Charles II. was proclaimed in Barnstaple, on which day Martin Blake began to use again the Book of Common Prayer, to the general satisfaction of his parishioners, only three of the Corporation being opposed to it, Nicholas Cooke, John Cooke, and Bartholomew Bisselend ; for the moderate Presbyterians, like Baxter, took no exception to it, and the Devon boroughs, even Totnes, an old Presbyterian stronghold, were willing to leave the resettlement of the Church to the King, for the Presbyterian system had never really taken root in the country. The old classical system laid down by Parliament had long been dead, and given place to the voluntary associations, and, as Monk had said in the Convention Parliament, a monarchial system in the State must be followed in the Church, and bishops brought in, and all were weary of the State ruling the details of Church Government. Certainly, in Barnstaple, there was a pretty general agreement that there must be a return to the Church's order as before the troubles, though a modified Episcopacy and a comprehension of Presbyterians was hoped for by many, and Blake was certainly of this party.

On November 3, 1660, John Gauden, the author of the "Eikon Basilike," and who had done more to bring about the Restoration than any other man save Monk, was elected Bishop of Exeter, in place of Brownrigg, who had died some eleven months before. On December 11, he was enthroned, and by the end of the year the Episcopal system was in working order again throughout the diocese.

Blake's old curate, James Smith, had been installed Archdeacon of Barnstaple nearly four months before, August 31, 1660, and at the first visitation held at Barnstaple, October 17, 1660, Blake was appointed to preach, and he took as his text the words : " For my brethren and companions' sakes, I will now say, Peace be within you, because of the house of the Lord our God I will seek thy good" (Ps. cxxii. 8, 9). The whole of this discourse is an earnest plea for peace and moderation. The sermon was afterwards printed by request, and published with a dedication to Bishop Gauden. The following year the Savoy Conference, from which much had been hoped for, came to nothing. Its report was that the

The Life of Martin Blake B.D.

Church's welfare, unity, and peace, were ends at which they were all agreed, but as to the means they could not come to any harmony.

But the spirit of Parliament was intensely opposed to any compromise with dissenters. As in Mary's reign it was argued that giving way to alterations had led to extremes and disunion, so now it was argued that all the troubles had been caused by dallying with Puritanism. The speaker of the House of Commons, in introducing the Act of Uniformity, said : "We cannot forget how the hedge being broken down the foxes and wolves did enter, the swine and other unclean beasts defiled the temple . . . it did not lend itself only to reform, but sought to root out Episcopal jurisdiction. Church ornaments were first taken away then the forms of common prayer were decried as superstitious, and in lieu thereof nothing or worse than nothing was introduced." However much compromise was desired by moderate men like Blake, who had petitioned the King on his restoration with other Devonshire ministers, expressing "their joy that to his zeal for the Protestant religion was joined a pitiful heart towards tender consciences, and hoping that he would protect the young and weak of the flock, who could not pace it with their older brethren," it was practically impossible. It was not that the restored Episcopalians returned to their livings

The Life of Martin Blake B.D.

with savagely accentuated feelings of triumph and long-nourished hopes of revenge after their inhuman persecutions, but it was rather that English Puritanism had been warped from its original position and true nature by the events of the years 1640-50, and the action of the Long Parliament. The fatal surrender of the Puritans in 1643 to Scottish Presbytery, their transient triumph from 1643-9, and their enforced and discontented acquiescence in Cromwell's religious arrangements from 1650 and onwards, had made it impossible for them to re-enter the Episcopal Church, at the Restoration, on anything like the old basis of English Puritanism. As we look at it now with cooler judgment, the surprise is not so much that compromise proved impossible, but that such a hope of it should have ever been entertained.

Comprehension could only have been achieved by the sacrifice of convictions on both sides, and this was a sacrifice their consciences would not allow them to make, and so the Church lost the services of men like the saintly Baxter, who refused a Bishoprick, Jonathan Hanmer of Bishop's Tawton, and many others of its most fervent spiritual element.

But beyond this, however much men like Blake would have been willing to concede, Parliament and the majority would have none of it. They saw that comprehension could only be achieved by the sacrifice of the first principles of the Church, and if these were thrown over there would be no Church left to restore.

The Act was passed, and on St Bartholomew, 1662, all the non-Episcopally ordained and intruded ministers withdrew, and with them some of the Episcopally ordained, who were conscientiously unable to accept the revised prayer-book. Amongst these was Jonathan Hanmer.

Both Blake and the new Bishop of Exeter, Seth Ward (who had succeeded Gauden, translated to Worcester May 23), used every endeavour to persuade him to conform; for Hanmer was practically far more in agreement with the Church than with the extreme non-conformists. So late as 1657 we find him publishing a treatise on Confirmation as being the ancient way of completing Church membership—while Confirmation had been a point to which the Puritans had specially objected at the Savoy Conference; but Hanmer was determined not to sign, and, though the Bishop showed him every consideration, he had to leave. Blake was excessively distressed that all his efforts on Hanmer's behalf were unavailing. "He helped me in my troubles," he said, "and yet now, I seem to be able to do nothing for him." To Hanmer he said: "My heart bleeds wherever I see you, to think that such a person should be cast out." In one point, however, Blake's efforts were successful. Fermor Pepys, the new incumbent of Bishop's Tawton, and several parishioners had withheld the late vicar's dues up to the time of his leaving. Blake on hearing this, brought the matter before the Bishop, and after relating Hanmer's standing by him in his troubles, said that Hanmer was not one of the non-ordained intruding sectaries, but a minister of the English Church, who was unable conscientiously to sign a consent to a prayer-book that differed from that to which he had subscribed when he was ordained, and his efforts were successful, the Bishop sending the following citation to the vicar and parishioners, who were withholding Hanmer's dues :—

" We desire you forthwith to make satisfaction to Mr Jonathan Hanmer in his past demands. As also to admonish you that if you shall delay to do it, such a course will speedily be taken against you, as will be very much to your prejudice. Withal adding as your performance of your duty in doing right to Mr Hanmer upon this my brotherly desire and admonition shall be now taken by me as an act of kindness and respect, so if this entreaty de despis'd and you shall persist (contrary to the laws of God and of this kingdom) to detain his dues from him I shall think myself obliged in all just and legal ways to

The Life of Martin Blake B.D.

discountenance you by taking care (within the compass of my jurisdiction) that the law be strictly executed upon you when you shall be required.

"SETH EXON."

Hanmer after his withdrawal from communion with the Church, retired into private life at Barnstaple till 1672, when "on the Indulgence," he formed a congregation known as the Castle Meeting, and was buried in the Parish Churchyard on December 21, 1687, aged 81; by his wife Katherine, daughter of Mr John Strange of Bideford, he had a family of nine children, most of whom predeceased him.

Of the latter years of Blake's ministry at Barnstaple, there is little to be said. Five years after the Restoration he was appointed a Canon or Prebendary of the Cathedral Church at Exeter (June 3, 1665).

During the declining years of his life, he began to gather together materials for an autobiography, and jot down particulars of his persecutions and conflicts with the lecturers; and it is from these somewhat disjointed papers that this account has been mainly drawn up.

During the last four years of his life, he had the assistance of a curate, the Rev. J. Tickell, from which it seems that Blake maintained his reputation as a moderate and reconciler of

The Life of Martin Blake B.D.

differences to the last; for Tickell had been one of the non-conforming clergy in 1662, and only conformed some years after at Blake's persuasion. To the last the old vicar performed his duties, and died at the age of seventy-eight, and was buried in the Parish Church by the south chancel wall, September 13, 1673, his second wife having predeceased him a little more than a year.

The only will he left was one made twenty-two years before, during the troubles, and just after the death of his beloved daughter; it is a holograph one, and somewhat quaint, and so I give a somewhat full abstract. It contains many erasures and interlineations :—

"In the Name of the most Holy and Glorious Trinitie God Blessed for ever Amen.

"I Martin Blake of Barnstaple in the County of Devon Clerk being at present (I thank God) sound in body and of perfect memorie doe hereby constitute my last will and testament in manner and forme following

"First I most humbly comend my soule into the hands of my creator hoping to be saved only by the merits and alsufficient satisfaction of my Blessed Saviour Jesus Christ.

"Secondly for my body I desire it may be decently interred in the Chancell of the Church at Barstaple as near the south wall as may be

The Life of Martin Blake B.D.

that being the place where my father my wife
and two of my children all of pretious memorie
were layd.

"Thirdly for my religion that I may leave
behind me some fitting testimonie therof especialie
in this lamentable varietie of new and strange
opinions now on foot I doe declair it is the same
which is expressed in the Doctrine of the Church
of England contayned in the 39 Articles and in
reference to that I doe professe with St Hierome
' In eadem religione in qua infans baptizatus sum
senescens morior' being by God's blessing
arrived to the full age of 58 yeeres during w^{ch}
tyme though I must confess to my own just
reproof that I have done many things wch I should
not have done and have left undone more wch I
should have done; yet I humbly thank God for
his grace through Jesus Christ I have so lived
'that I am not ashamed to live longer nor yet
afraid to dye seing I serve a good master.

"Lastly as for my temporall estate I blesse and
magnifie the Name of God for that portion of
meanes wch of his bounteous goodness and without any desert of mine he hath bestowed upon
me I doe hereby ordaine and nominate my dearly
beloved son John Blake Executor not doubting
but that he will really pay my lawful debts as well
as those legacies which by this my last will or
otherwise in a codicill annexed hereunto shall

The Life of Martin Blake B.D.

appear, the better to enable him thereunto I give and bequeath to him over and above that portion of my inheritance which he is to enjoy as my heire the full remainder of that my estate and inheritance in a certain tenement in West Buckland now in the possession of one James Brayly which I have in lease by the grant of Mr John Delbridge my father in law deceased as also my bookes and all my other goods and chattels which I shall leave in ready coyne. And for his assistance I do name and appoint as overseers my dear brother Mr Nicholas Blake of London merchant and my endeared son in law Mr Richard Musgrave of Nettlecombe gent, and to the sayd overseers I give not for a reward of their paynes but as a token of my love 40s to each of them to buy rings.

"Thus beseeching Almighty God to preserve and bless this whole Church and State by making up the unhappy breaches and distractions thereof and settling righteousness and peace in both and withall heartily forgiving all men who have offended me though to persecution as I desire to be in like sort forgiven of those whom I have offended and that God would mercifully forgive us all. I have thereunto set my hand and seale the . . . day of September in the year of our Lord God 1651°.

"MARTIN BLAKE."

The Life of Martin Blake B.D.

The will has no seal, though one is spoken of in it, neither any witnesses; nor can any trace of the annexed codicil spoken of be found, though a careful search has been made in the Probate Court archives. It would seem that the will was a draft made and signed by Blake just after his daughter Joan's death and never formally completed.

It was proved December '31' 1673, by John Blake the vicar's only surviving child.

I have endeavoured to trace as far as possible **the** descendants of Martin Blake. His son John was baptized at Barnstaple, June 26, 1631, and married January 4, 1665-6; at Barnstaple, his cousin Mary Downe, elder daughter of the Reverend Richard Downe, D.D., Rector of Tawstock and Marwood (1632 to 1652) by Mary, daughter of Sir Robert Lovet of Corfe, and sister of the Countess of Bath.

John Blake settled at Barnstaple, of which town he was Mayor in 1686, he had by his wife three sons: Richard, born 1671, Martin, born 1675, and John, born 1678-9; and two daughters: Elizabeth, born 1673, and Joan, born 1682. John Blake, Sen., was buried June 13, 1696, and Mrs Blake February 14, 1699-1700

Of John Blake's sons Richard and Martin died without issue; the third son, John, married at Goodleigh, May 22, 1715, Agnes Budd, daughter

The Life of Martin Blake B.D.

of Arthur Budd of Willsleigh in the parish of Landkey. They had an only son, Martin, baptized April 15, 1716, at Goodleigh, in whom the male line of the vicar's descendants ended. The elder daughter of John Blake, Sen., married at Barnstaple July 1, 1695, John Lee, gent., of Barnstaple, by whom she had two sons and two daughters, her daughter Mary baptized April 4, 1697, the only survivor married as his second wife, April 27, 1720; Rev. Robert Luck, Vicar of West Downe and Buckland Brewer, and master of Barnstaple Grammar School. Mrs Luck died without issue and was buried at Barnstaple July 7, 1748.

The younger daughter, Joan, married at Charles, August .5, 1701, Lewis Gregory, Town-Clerk and Mayor of Barnstaple, son of the Rev. George Gregory, Rector of Charles, by Mary, daughter of Christopher Wood of Ashridge, by whom she had George, baptized December 29, 1702; John, baptized October 14, 1704, buried November 1708; Mary and Anne. George, the only surviving son, was Rector of Combemartin and Instow. He married Thomazine, daughter of William Reynolds, M.D., of Barnstaple, and had by her three sons and six daughters; Lewis, John, and Martin Blake, Joan, Thomasine, Mary Lee, Federetta, Ann, and Elizabeth. Lewis, baptized January 21, 1729-30, was an attorney at Dunster,

The Life of Martin Blake B.D.

married Dorothy, daughter of Charles Marshall, and had an only son, Charles Gregory, a captain in the Royal Navy in 1820; Martin Blake Gregory, died in 1760; John I cannot trace; five of the daughters married and left children : Thomasine to John Robins, gent., Mary Lee to Samuel Johns, Lieut. R. N., Federetta to Francis Smith, Esq., of the Island of Jamaica, Elizabeth to Henry Downe, Esq., of Borough, and Ann to John Griffiths. Of these, probably many descendants are still living; also, perhaps, of Mary, daughter of Lewis and Joan Gregory, who married first, Nathaniel Moore of Barnstaple, second, her cousin John, son of Samuel Gregory of Braunton, and Ann, her sister, who married John Drake. Mary Luck, Blake's great granddaughter, made an effort to revive the family name. By her will, dated June 26, 1741, she left all her real estate to Dr William Barbor and John Drake, husband of her kinswoman Ann Drake, upon trust, for the benefit of her husband for life, and after his death, for Martin Blake Gregory, third and youngest son of George Gregory, clerk, and heirs of his body, provided that within two years of her husband's death, or of attaining the age of twenty-one, he obtained an Act of Parliament for changing his name to Blake; in default for John Gregory, second son of George Gregory, on like condition; in default for any future-born son of George Gregory on like condition; in default for the first and every son of Ann Drake, senior, on like condition; in default upon trust for Lewis Gregory on like conditions; in default for Mary Lee Gregory, and heirs of her body. Administration was granted to the father of Martin Blake Gregory, December 14, 1749, Dr Barbor and John Drake having renounced, but I cannot find that its conditions were fulfilled. Martin Blake Gregory was buried March 3, 1760. I find his elder brother and all his sisters living in 1793, but cannot trace them any farther, and as far as I am aware, no descendant has revived the name of Blake. It survived, however, in the line of the descendants of his brother, Nicholas, for many generations, and may possibly do so still; his son Thomas Blake, matriculated at Exeter College, Oxford, in 1669, became Rector of Alwington, Devon, in 1677, on the death of his uncle, Rev. Thomas Mathews, and had four sons, the eldest of whom, George, fellow of Exeter College, Oxford, succeeded his father as Rector of Alwington, and was buried there, June 8, 1763; another son, Thomas Blake, was a goldsmith at Exeter, the others I cannot trace.

No tombstone or memorial now marks the last resting-place of Martin Blake, Vicar of Barnstaple, but he will be ever remembered by the

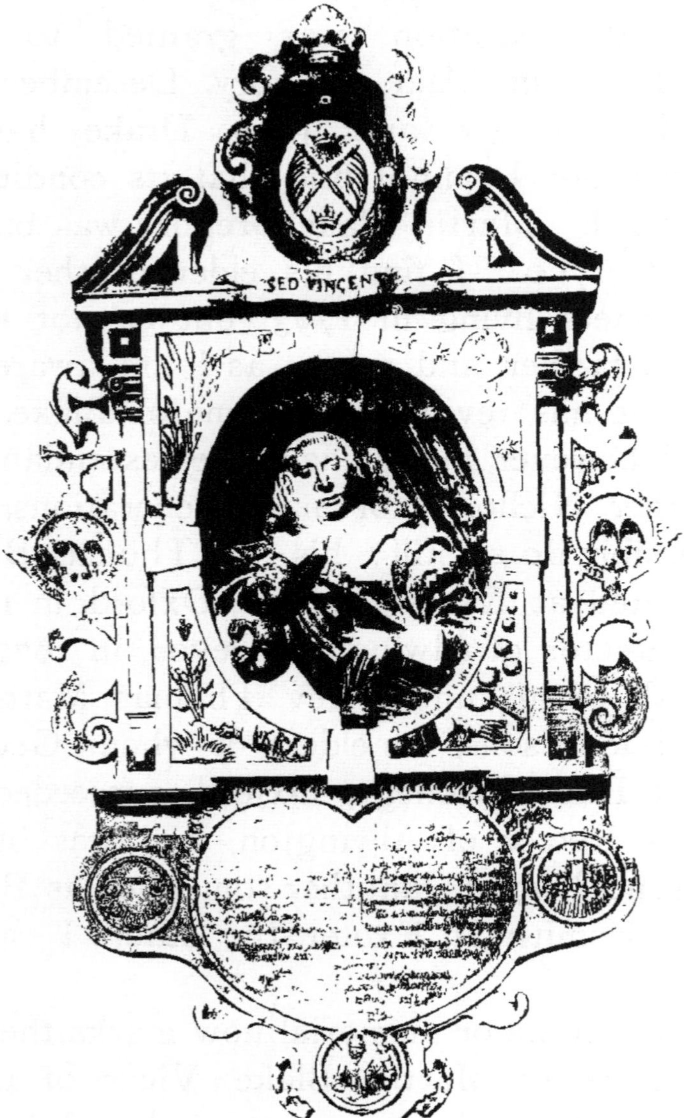
SED VINCENT

THE BLAKE MONUMENT

curious and remarkable monument which the vicar himself erected " To the honour and glorie of God and in pretiouse memorie of my deare sonne Nicholas Blake who fell asleep in Christ Feb. xij. An: Do: MDCXXXiiij. Aetatis suae ix°." No visitor to the Church of St Peter at Barnstaple should come away without examining it, or if he has patience, without hearing the quaint lecture which the dear old verger loves to give, embellished though it be with somewhat apochryphal details, for the monument is not only a good example of the period, but a pictorial representation of the vicar's faith, fears, foes, and family. It was erected in the year 1646, during the vicar's first persecution, when he was silenced, and there was no other minister in Barnstaple, and he appears to have devised it as much in allusion to his own position as to his children. It has been removed from its original position in the chancel to the south chancel aisle, where it can be better seen and has been twice restored in the process of which some of the words in the inscription have been altered.

It is an alabaster monument of the renaissance style, consisting of an oblong frame between two Ionic columns, with the usual surroundings of this style.

In an oval recess in the centre, under a curtained canopy, is the half-length figure of a

The Life of Martin Blake B.D.

boy in the dress of the period, his head reclining on his right hand, the elbow resting on a skull, the left hand grasping a bible. In the four corners, between the oval and oblong frames, are coloured sculptured illustrations of Latin texts :—

(1) "Cum fœnere et flore reddit"—A hand sowing corn with ears springing up.

(2) "Splendebunt ut stellæ erynt sicut Angeli"—A cherub surmounting four stars.

(3) "Ut flos simul ac egressus est succiditur"—A lily in bloom, a hand stretching forth to pluck it, and cast it into the fire.

(4) "Dies Hominis palmaris et homo bulla"—A hand stretched out representing a span—A pipe with a series of bubbles blown from it.

Medallions to the right and left :—

(1) Two children bearing palm branches, William Blake, Mary Blake—"Sequuntur Agnum."

(2) Two children bearing palm branches, Elizabeth Blake, Agness Blake—"Non esurient amplius neq sitient."

Under the figure on a tablet is the inscription to his son given above, and the verses :—

"Few years with many Graces (more by far
Than to such tender age accustomed are)
God lent thee here, but may it be a child
Of such sweet hopes so virtuous and so mild

The Life of Martin Blake B.D.

Should passe so soone away and not partake
That promise of long life wch God did make
Nay ; May that promise hold for although here
Thy Pilgrimage was short, thy joys elsewhere
Doe never die and thy whole man shall stand
Crowned ere long with Life i' th' promised Land
W^{ch} Life whilst God for thee vouchsafes to keep
Here he was pleased to lay thy Corps asleep."

"Requiesce mi fili ! requiesce in pace ! cupit etiam dissolvi et tecum esse cum Christo pater tuus utrinque coarctatus Martinus Blake S. T. B. hujusque ecclesiæ Barnestapulensis pastor indignus, tempore opportuno etiam reversurus."

Below this, in a medallion, is a figure of Martin Blake himself, represented as wearing a beard, and with a skull cap, and wearing a gown, his hands pointing right and left to two medallions :—

(1) A glory and five cherubs—"Quantum ad hoc mihi lucrum est mori."
(2) The interior of a church, with the congregation standing before an empty pulpit—"Quantum ad hos permanere in carne magis necessarium."

On the top is a medallion having, instead of armorial bearings, in an oval azure, two palm branches, with two sceptres crossed between two coronets and a crown in place of a crest, and the inscription—"Reposita est atque dabitur sed vincenti." This inscription should be—"Sed vincenti," but for him who conquers ; "reposita

The Life of Martin Blake B.D.

est," there is laid up—the palm of victory and crown; "atque dabitur," and it shall be given.

Local tradition says the empty pulpit represents the fact that Blake was dragged from his pulpit by two soldiers during the Commonwealth. This is undoubtedly untrue; the allusion is to the congregation coming, but Blake not being allowed to preach, and there being no other minister. The tradition, doubtless, had its birth in the fact that Blake was forcibly dragged from his house by two soldiers, during his second persecution as I have already related.

In this story of Martin Blake I have only attempted to give an account of such parts of the civil history of the town with which Blake was directly connected, and as full an ecclesiastical history of Barnstaple during the period of his incumbency as I am able; but in so doing I have carefully refrained from telling again anything in its municipal history that has been related by previous writers, and even Dr Walker's long accounts of Blake's sufferings have been passed over, or rather, I have re-edited, and I trust with freedom from bias, the papers from which Dr Walker's story was compiled, supplementing it with fuller details, and it is an attempt to gather together in a connected form, and with some chronological order, such of Martin Blake's life, letters, and thoughts, as have been preserved in

The Life of Martin Blake B.D.

a few disjointed and widely scattered papers, and
as such, I trust it will be not only a contribution
to the ecclesiastical and parochial history of my
native town, but also of some interest to a wider
circle, as recording the *ipsissima verba* and inner
thoughts of a Devonshire parson during a period
that, lying as it does, midway between mediæval
and modern life, will be always one of the most
fascinating pages in English history.

INDEX

INDEX

Index

M

Index

NOTICE

Those who possess old letters, documents, correspondence, MSS., scraps of autobiography, and also miniatures and portraits, relating to persons and matters historical, literary, political and social, should communicate with Mr. John Lane, The Bodley Head, Vigo Street, London, W., who will at all times be pleased to give his advice and assistance, either as to their preservation or publication.

LIVING MASTERS OF MUSIC

An Illustrated Series of Monographs dealing with Contemporary Musical Life, and including Representatives of all Branches of the Art. Edited by ROSA NEWMARCH. Crown 8vo. Cloth. 2s. 6d. net each volume.

HENRY J. WOOD. By ROSA NEWMARCH.

SIR EDWARD ELGAR. By R. J. BUCKLEY.

JOSEPH JOACHIM. By J. A. FULLER MAITLAND.

EDWARD MACDOWELL. By L. GILMAN.

EDVARD GRIEG. By H. T. FINCK.

THEODOR LESCHETIZKY. By A. HULLAH.

GIACOMO PUCCINI. By WAKELING DRY.

ALFRED BRUNEAU. By ARTHUR HERVEY.

IGNAZ PADEREWSKI. By E. A. BAUGHAN.

RICHARD STRAUSS. By A. KALISCH.

CLAUDE DEBUSSY. By FRANZ LIEBICH.

STARS OF THE STAGE

A Series of Illustrated Biographies of the Leading Actors, Actresses, and Dramatists. Edited by J. T. GREIN. Crown 8vo. 2s. 6d. each net.

₊ *It was Schiller who said: " Twine no wreath for the actor, since his work is oral and ephemeral." "Stars of the Stage" may in some degree remove this reproach. There are hundreds of thousands of playgoers, and both editor and publisher think it reasonable to assume that a considerable number of these would like to know something about actors, actresses, and dramatists, whose work they nightly applaud. Each volume will be carefully illustrated, and as far as text, printing, and paper are concerned will be a notable book. Great care has been taken in selecting the biographers, who in most cases have already accumulated much appropriate material.*

First Volumes.

ELLEN TERRY. By CHRISTOPHER ST. JOHN.

HERBERT BEERBOHM TREE. By MRS. GEORGE CRAN.

W. S. GILBERT. By EDITH A. BROWNE.

CHAS. WYNDHAM. By FLORENCE TEIGNMOUTH SHORE.

GEORGE BERNARD SHAW. By G. K. CHESTERTON.

A CATALOGUE OF
MEMOIRS, BIOGRAPHIES, ETC.

WORKS UPON NAPOLEON

NAPOLEON & THE INVASION OF ENGLAND:
The Story of the Great Terror, 1797–1805. By H. F. B. WHEELER and A. M. BROADLEY. With upwards of 100 Full-page Illustrations reproduced from Contemporary Portraits, Prints, etc.; eight in Colour. Two Volumes. 32s. net.

Outlook.—"The book is not merely one to be ordered from the library; it should be purchased, kept on an accessible shelf, and constantly studied by all Englishmen who love England."

DUMOURIEZ AND THE DEFENCE OF ENGLAND AGAINST NAPOLEON. By J. HOLLAND ROSE, Litt.D. (Cantab.), Author of "The Life of Napoleon," and A. M. BROADLEY, joint-author of "Napoleon and the Invasion of England." Illustrated with numerous Portraits, Maps, and Facsimiles. Demy 8vo. 21s. net.

THE FALL OF NAPOLEON. By OSCAR BROWNING, M.A., Author of "The Boyhood and Youth of Napoleon." With numerous Full-page Illustrations. Demy 8vo (9 × 5¾ inches). 12s. 6d. net.

Spectator.—"Without doubt Mr. Oscar Browning has produced a book which should have its place in any library of Napoleonic literature."
Truth.—"Mr. Oscar Browning has made not the least, but the most of the romantic material at his command for the story of the fall of the greatest figure in history."

THE BOYHOOD & YOUTH OF NAPOLEON,
1769–1793. Some Chapters on the early life of Bonaparte. By OSCAR BROWNING, M.A. With numerous Illustrations, Portraits, etc. Crown 8vo. 5s. net.

Daily News.—"Mr. Browning has with patience, labour, careful study, and excellent taste given us a very valuable work, which will add materially to the literature on this most fascinating of human personalities."

THE LOVE AFFAIRS OF NAPOLEON. By JOSEPH TURQUAN. Translated from the French by JAMES L. MAY. With 32 Full-page Illustrations. Demy 8vo (9 × 5½ inches). 12s. 6d. net.

THE DUKE OF REICHSTADT (NAPOLEON II.)

By EDWARD DE WERTHEIMER. Translated from the German. With numerous Illustrations. Demy 8vo. 21*s*. net. (Second Edition.)

Times.—"A most careful and interesting work which presents the first complete and authoritative account of the life of this unfortunate Prince."

Westminster Gazette.—"This book, admirably produced, reinforced by many additional portraits, is a solid contribution to history and a monument of patient, well-applied research."

NAPOLEON'S CONQUEST OF PRUSSIA, 1806.

By F. LORAINE PETRE. With an Introduction by FIELD-MARSHAL EARL ROBERTS, V.C., K.G., etc. With Maps, Battle Plans, Portraits, and 16 Full-page Illustrations. Demy 8vo (9 × 5¾ inches). 12*s*. 6*d*. net.

Scotsman.—"Neither too concise, nor too diffuse, the book is eminently readable It is the best work in English on a somewhat circumscribed subject."

Outlook.—"Mr. Petre has visited the battlefields and read everything, and his monograph is a model of what military history, handled with enthusiasm and literary ability, can be."

NAPOLEON'S CAMPAIGN IN POLAND, 1806–

1807. A Military History of Napoleon's First War with Russia, verified from unpublished official documents. By F. LORAINE PETRE. With 16 Full-page Illustrations, Maps, and Plans. New Edition. Demy 8vo (9 × 5¾ inches). 12*s*. 6*d*. net.

Army and Navy Chronicle —"We welcome a second edition of this valuable work. . . . Mr Loraine Petre is an authority on the wars of the great Napoleon, and has brought the greatest care and energy into his studies of the subject."

NAPOLEON AND THE ARCHDUKE

CHARLES. A History of the Franco-Austrian Campaign in the Valley of the Danube in 1809. By F. LORAINE PETRE. With 8 Illustrations and 6 sheets of Maps and Plans. Demy 8vo (9 × 5¾ inches). 12*s*. 6*d*. net.

RALPH HEATHCOTE. Letters of a Diplomatist

During the Time of Napoleon, Giving an Account of the Dispute between the Emperor and the Elector of Hesse. By COUNTESS GUNTHER GROBEN. With Numerous Illustrations. Demy 8vo (9 × 5¾ inches). 12*s*. 6*d*. net.

*** *Ralph Heathcote, the son of an English father and an Alsatian mother, was for some time in the English diplomatic service as first secretary to Mr. Brook Taylor, minister at the Court of Hesse, and on one occasion found himself very near to making history. Napoleon became persuaded that Taylor was implicated in a plot to procure his assassination, and insisted on his dismissal from the Hessian Court. As Taylor refused to be dismissed, the incident at one time seemed likely to result to the Elector in the loss of his throne Heathcote came into contact with a number of notable people, including the Miss Berrys, with whom he assures his mother he is not in love. On the whole, there is much interesting material for lovers of old letters and journals.*

MEMOIRS OF THE COUNT DE CARTRIE.

A record of the extraordinary events in the life of a French Royalist during the war in La Vendée, and of his flight to Southampton, where he followed the humble occupation of gardener. With an introduction by FRÉDÉRIC MASSON, Appendices and Notes by PIERRE AMÉDÉE PICHOT, and other hands, and numerous Illustrations, including a Photogravure Portrait of the Author. Demy 8vo. 12s. 6d. net.

Daily News.—"We have seldom met with a human document which has interested us so much."

THE JOURNAL OF JOHN MAYNE DURING

A TOUR ON THE CONTINENT UPON ITS REOPENING AFTER THE FALL OF NAPOLEON, 1814. Edited by his Grandson, JOHN MAYNE COLLES. With 16 Illustrations. Demy 8vo (9 × 5¾ inches). 12s. 6d. net.

WOMEN OF THE SECOND EMPIRE.

Chronicles of the Court of Napoleon III. By FRÉDÉRIC LOLIÉE. With an introduction by RICHARD WHITEING and 53 full-page Illustrations, 3 in Photogravure. Demy 8vo. 21s. net.

Standard.—"M. Frédéric Loliée has written a remarkable book, vivid and pitiless in its description of the intrigue and dare-devil spirit which flourished unchecked at the French Court. . . . Mr. Richard Whiteing's introduction is written with restraint and dignity."

LOUIS NAPOLEON AND THE GENESIS OF

THE SECOND EMPIRE. By F. H. CHEETHAM. With Numerous Illustrations. Demy 8vo (9 × 5¾ inches). 16s. net.

MEMOIRS OF MADEMOISELLE DES

ÉCHEROLLES. Translated from the French by MARIE CLOTHILDE BALFOUR. With an Introduction by G. K. FORTESCUE, Portraits, etc. 5s. net.

Liverpool Mercury.—". . . this absorbing book. . . . The work has a very decided historical value. The translation is excellent, and quite notable in the preservation of idiom."

JANE AUSTEN'S SAILOR BROTHERS. Being

the life and Adventures of Sir Francis Austen, G.C.B., Admiral of the Fleet, and Rear-Admiral Charles Austen. By J. H. and E. C. HUBBACK. With numerous Illustrations. Demy 8vo. 12s. 6d. net.

Morning Post.—". . . May be welcomed as an important addition to Austeniana . . .; it is besides valuable for its glimpses of life in the Navy, its illustrations of the feelings and sentiments of naval officers during the period that preceded and that which followed the great battle of just one century ago, the battle which won so much but which cost us—Nelson."

SOME WOMEN LOVING AND LUCKLESS.

By Teodor de Wyzewa. Translated from the French by C. H. Jeffreson, M.A. With Numerous Illustrations. Demy 8vo (9 × 5¾ inches). 7s. 6d. net.

POETRY AND PROGRESS IN RUSSIA. By

Rosa Newmarch. With 6 full-page Portraits. Demy 8vo. 7s. 6d. net.

Standard —"Distinctly a book that should be read . . . pleasantly written and well informed.''

GIOVANNI BOCCACCIO : A BIOGRAPHICAL

STUDY. By Edward Hutton. With a Photogravure Frontispiece and numerous other Illustrations. Demy 8vo (9 × 5¾ inches). 16s. net.

THE LIFE OF PETER ILICH TCHAIKOVSKY

(1840–1893). By his Brother, Modeste Tchaikovsky. Edited and abridged from the Russian and German Editions by Rosa Newmarch. With Numerous Illustrations and Facsimiles and an Introduction by the Editor. Demy 8vo. 7s. 6d. net. Second edition.

The Times —"A most illuminating commentary on Tchaikovsky's music."
World.—"One of the most fascinating self-revelations by an artist which has been given to the world. The translation is excellent, and worth reading for its own sake."
Contemporary Review.—"The book's appeal is, of course, primarily to the music-lover ; but there is so much of human and literary interest in it, such intimate revelation of a singularly interesting personality, that many who have never come under the spell of the Pathetic Symphony will be strongly attracted by what is virtually the spiritual autobiography of its composer. High praise is due to the translator and editor for the literary skill with which she has prepared the English version of this fascinating work . . There have been few collections of letters published within recent years that give so vivid a portrait of the writer as that presented to us in these pages."

COKE OF NORFOLK AND HIS FRIENDS :

The Life of Thomas William Coke, First Earl of Leicester of the second creation, containing an account of his Ancestry, Surroundings, Public Services, and Private Friendships, and including many Unpublished Letters from Noted Men of his day, English and American. By A. M. W. Stirling. With 20 Photogravure and upwards of 40 other Illustrations reproduced from Contemporary Portraits, Prints, etc. Demy 8vo. 2 vols. 32s. net.

The Times.—"We thank Mr. Stirling for one of the most interesting memoirs of recent years"
Daily Telegraph.—"A very remarkable literary performance. Mrs Stirling has achieved a resurrection. She has fashioned a picture of a dead and forgotten past and brought before our eyes with the vividness of breathing existence the life of our English ancestors of the eighteenth century."
Pall Mall Gazette —"A work of no common interest ; in fact, a work which may almost be called unique."
Evening Standard —"One of the most interesting biographies we have read for years."

THE LIFE OF SIR HALLIDAY MACART-
NEY, K.C.M.G., Commander of Li Hung Chang's trained
force in the Taeping Rebellion, founder of the first Chinese
Arsenal, Secretary to the first Chinese Embassy to Europe.
Secretary and Councillor to the Chinese Legation in London for
thirty years. By DEMETRIUS C. BOULGER, Author of the
"History of China," the "Life of Gordon," etc. With Illus-
trations. Demy 8vo. Price 21s. net.

Daily Graphic.—"It is safe to say that few readers will be able to put down the book without feeling the better for having read it . . . not only full of personal interest, but
tells us much that we never knew before on some not unimportant details."

DEVONSHIRE CHARACTERS AND STRANGE
EVENTS. By S. BARING-GOULD, M.A., Author of "Yorkshire
Oddities," etc. With 58 Illustrations. Demy 8vo. 21s. net.

Daily News.—"A fascinating series . . . the whole book is rich in human interest. It is
by personal touches, drawn from traditions and memories, that the dead men surrounded
by the curious panoply of their time, are made to live again in Mr. Baring-Gould's pages."

CORNISH CHARACTERS AND STRANGE
EVENTS. By S. BARING-GOULD. Demy 8vo. 21s. net.

THE HEART OF GAMBETTA. Translated
from the French of FRANCIS LAUR by VIOLETTE MONTAGU.
With an Introduction by JOHN MACDONALD, Portraits and other
Illustrations. Demy 8vo. 7s. 6d. net.

Daily Telegraph—"It is Gambetta pouring out his soul to Léonie Leon, the strange,
passionate, masterful demagogue, who wielded the most persuasive oratory of modern
times, acknowledging his idol, his inspiration, his Egeria."

THE MEMOIRS OF ANN, LADY FANSHAWE.
Written by Lady Fanshawe. With Extracts from the Correspondence of Sir Richard Fanshawe. Edited by H. C. FANSHAWE.
With 38 Full-page Illustrations, including four in Photogravure
and one in Colour. Demy 8vo. 16s. net.

*** *This Edition has been printed direct from the original manuscript in the possession
of the Fanshawe Family, and Mr. H. C. Fanshawe contributes numerous notes which
form a running commentary on the text. Many famous pictures are reproduced, includ-*

THE LIFE OF JOAN OF ARC. By ANATOLE FRANCE. A Translation by WINIFRED STEPHENS. With 8 Illustrations. Demy 8vo (9 × 5¾ inches). 2 vols. Price 25s. net.

THE DAUGHTER OF LOUIS XVI. Marie-Thérèse-Charlotte of France, Duchesse D'Angoulême. By. G. LENOTRE. With 13 Full-page Illustrations. Demy 8vo. Price 10s. 6d. net.

WITS, BEAUX, AND BEAUTIES OF THE GEORGIAN ERA. By JOHN FYVIE, author of "Some Famous Women of Wit and Beauty," "Comedy Queens of the Georgian Era," etc. With a Photogravure Portrait and numerous other Illustrations. Demy 8vo (9 × 5¾ inches). 12s. 6d. net.

LADIES FAIR AND FRAIL. Sketches of the Demi-monde during the Eighteenth Century. By HORACE BLEACKLEY, author of "The Story of a Beautiful Duchess." With 1 Photogravure and 15 other Portraits reproduced from contemporary sources. Demy 8vo (9 × 5½ inches). 12s. 6d. net.

MADAME DE MAINTENON : Her Life and Times, 1635–1719. By C. C. DYSON. With 1 Photogravure Plate and 16 other Illustrations. Demy 8vo (9 × 5¾ inches). 12s. 6d. net.

DR. JOHNSON AND MRS. THRALE. By A. M. BROADLEY. With an Introductory Chapter by THOMAS SECCOMBE. With 24 Illustrations from rare originals, including a reproduction in colours of the Fellowes Miniature of Mrs. Piozzi by Roche, and a Photogravure of Harding's sepia drawing of Dr. Johnson. Demy 8vo (9 × 5¾ inches). 12s. 6d. net.

THE DAYS OF THE DIRECTOIRE. By ALFRED ALLINSON, M.A. With 48 Full-page Illustrations, including many illustrating the dress of the time. Demy 8vo (9 × 5¾ inches). 16s. net.

HUBERT AND JOHN VAN EYCK : Their Life
and Work. By W. H. JAMES WEALE. With 41 Photogravure
and 95 Black and White Reproductions. Royal 4to. £5 5s. net.

SIR MARTIN CONWAY'S NOTE.

Nearly half a century has passed since Mr. W. H. James Weale, then resident at Bruges, began that long series of patient investigations into the history of Netherlandish art which was destined to earn so rich a harvest. When he began work Memlinc was still called Hemling, and was fabled to have arrived at Bruges as a wounded soldier. The van Eycks were little more than legendary heroes. Roger Van der Weyden was little more than a name. Most of the other great Netherlandish artists were either wholly forgotten or named only in connection with paintings with which they had nothing to do Mr. Weale discovered Gerard David, and disentangled his principal works from Memlinc's, with which they were then confused

VINCENZO FOPPA OF BRESCIA, FOUNDER OF
THE LOMBARD SCHOOL, HIS LIFE AND WORK. By CONSTANCE
JOCELYN FFOULKES and MONSIGNOR RODOLFO MAJOCCHI, D.D.,
Rector of the Collegio Borromeo, Pavia. Based on research in the
Archives of Milan, Pavia, Brescia, and Genoa, and on the study
of all his known works. With over 100 Illustrations, many in
Photogravure, and 100 Documents. Royal 4to. £3. 11s. 6d. net.

⁎⁎⁎ No complete Life of Vincenzo Foppa has ever been written. an omission which seems almost inexplicable in these days of over-production in the matter of biographies of painters, and of subjects relating to the art of Italy. The object of the authors of this book has been to present a true picture of the master's life based upon the testimony of records in Italian archives. The authors have unearthed a large amount of new material relating to Foppa, one of the most interesting facts brought to light being that he lived for twenty-three years longer than was formerly supposed. The illustrations will include several pictures by Foppa hitherto unknown in the history of art.

MEMOIRS OF THE DUKES OF URBINO.
Illustrating the Arms, Art and Literature of Italy from 1440 to
1630. By JAMES DENNISTOUN of Dennistoun. A New Edition
edited by EDWARD HUTTON, with upwards of 100 Illustrations.
Demy 8vo. 3 vols. 42s. net.

⁎⁎⁎ For many years this great book has been out o, print although it still remains the chief authority upon the Duchy of Urbino from the beginning of the fifteenth century. Mr. Hutton has carefully edited the whole work, leaving the text substantially the same, but adding a large number of new notes, comments and references Wherever possible the reader is directed to original sources. Every sort of work has been laid under contribution to illustrate the text, and bibliographies have been supplied on many subjects. Besides these notes the book acquires a new value on account of the mass of illustrations which it now contains, thus adding a pictorial comment to an historical and critical one.

THE PHILOSOPHY OF LONG LIFE. By
JEAN FINOT. A Translation by HARRY ROBERTS. Demy 8vo.
(9 × 5¾ inches). 7s. 6d. net.

⁎⁎⁎ This is a translation of a book which has attained to the position of a classic. It has already been translated into almost every language, and has, in France, gone into fourteen editions in the course of a few years. The book is an exhaustive one, and although based on science and philosophy it is in no sense abstruse or remote from general interest. It deals with life as embodied not only in man and in the animal and vegetable worlds, but in all that great world of (as the author holds) misnamed "inanimate" nature as well. For M. Finot argues that all things have life and consciousness, and that a solidarity exists which brings together all beings and so-called things. He sets himself to work to show that life, in its philosophic conception, is an elemental force, and durable as nature herself.

THE DIARY OF A LADY-IN-WAITING. By

LADY CHARLOTTE BURY. Being the Diary Illustrative of the Times of George the Fourth. Interspersed with original Letters from the late Queen Caroline and from various other distinguished persons. New edition. Edited, with an Introduction, by A. FRANCIS STEUART. With numerous portraits. Two Vols. Demy 8vo. 21s. net

THE LAST JOURNALS OF HORACE WAL-

POLE. During the Reign of George III from 1771 to 1783. With Notes by DR. DORAN. Edited with an Introduction by A. FRANCIS STEUART, and containing numerous Portraits (2 in Photogravure) reproduced from contemporary Pictures, Engravings, etc. 2 vols. Uniform with "The Diary of a Lady-in-Waiting." Demy 8vo (9 × 5¾ inches). 25s. net.

JUNIPER HALL: Rendezvous of certain illus-

trious Personages during the French Revolution, including Alexander D'Arblay and Fanny Burney. Compiled by CONSTANCE HILL. With numerous Illustrations by ELLEN G. HILL, and reproductions from various Contemporary Portraits. Crown 8vo. 5s. net.

JANE AUSTEN: Her Homes and Her Friends.

By CONSTANCE HILL. Numerous Illustrations by ELLEN G. HILL, together with Reproductions from Old Portraits, etc. Cr. 8vo. 5s. net.

THE HOUSE IN ST. MARTIN'S STREET.

Being Chronicles of the Burney Family. By CONSTANCE HILL, Author of "Jane Austen, Her Home, and Her Friends," "Juniper Hall," etc. With numerous Illustrations by ELLEN G. HILL, and reproductions of Contemporary Portraits, etc. Demy 8vo. 21s. net.

STORY OF THE PRINCESS DES URSINS IN

SPAIN (Camarera-Mayor). By CONSTANCE HILL. With 12 Illustrations and a Photogravure Frontispiece. New Edition. Crown 8vo. 5s. net.

MARIA EDGEWORTH AND HER CIRCLE

IN THE DAYS OF BONAPARTE AND BOURBON. By CONSTANCE HILL. Author of "Jane Austen: Her Homes and Her Friends," "Juniper Hall," "The House in St. Martin's Street," etc. With numerous Illustrations by ELLEN G. HILL and Reproductions of Contemporary Portraits, etc. Demy 8vo

NEW LETTERS OF THOMAS CARLYLE.

Edited and Annotated by ALEXANDER CARLYLE, with Notes and an Introduction and numerous Illustrations. In Two Volumes. Demy 8vo. 25*s*. net.

Pall Mall Gazette.—"To the portrait of the man, Thomas, these letters do really add value; we can learn to respect and to like him the more for the genuine goodness of his personality."

Literary World.—"It is then Carlyle, the nobly filial son, we see in these letters; Carlyle, the generous and affectionate brother, the loyal and warm-hearted friend, . . . and above all, Carlyle as the tender and faithful lover of his wife."

Daily Telegraph.—"The letters are characteristic enough of the Carlyle we know: very picturesque and entertaining, full of extravagant emphasis, written, as a rule, at fever heat, eloquently rabid and emotional.'

NEW LETTERS AND MEMORIALS OF JANE

WELSH CARLYLE. A Collection of hitherto Unpublished Letters. Annotated by THOMAS CARLYLE, and Edited by ALEXANDER CARLYLE, with an Introduction by Sir JAMES CRICHTON BROWNE, M.D., LL.D., F.R.S., numerous Illustrations drawn in Lithography by T. R. WAY, and Photogravure Portraits from hitherto unreproduced Originals. In Two Volumes. Demy 8vo. 25*s*. net.

Westminster Gazette.—"Few letters in the language have in such perfection the qualities which good letters should possess. Frank, gay, brilliant, indiscreet, immensely clever, whimsical, and audacious, they reveal a character which, with whatever alloy of human infirmity, must endear itself to any reader of understanding."

World.—"Throws a deal of new light on the domestic relations of the Sage of Chelsea. They also contain the full text of Mrs. Carlyle's fascinating journal, and her own 'humorous and quaintly candid' narrative of her first love-affair."

THE LOVE LETTERS OF THOMAS CAR-

LYLE AND JANE WELSH. Edited by ALEXANDER CARLYLE, Nephew of THOMAS CARLYLE, editor of "New Letters and Memorials of Jane Welsh Carlyle," "New Letters of Thomas Carlyle," etc. With 2 Portraits in colour and numerous other Illustrations. Demy 8vo ($9 \times 5\frac{1}{2}$ inches). 2 vols. 25*s*. net.

CARLYLE'S FIRST LOVE. Margaret Gordon—

Lady Bannerman. An account of her Life, Ancestry and Homes; her Family and Friends. By R. C. ARCHIBALD. With 20 Portraits and Illustrations, including a Frontispiece in Colour. Demy 8vo ($9 \times 5\frac{3}{4}$ inches). 10*s*. 6*d*. net

ÉMILE ZOLA : NOVELIST AND REFORMER. An

Account of his Life, Work, and Influence. By E. A. VIZETELLY. With numerous Illustrations, Portraits, etc. Demy 8vo. 21*s*. net.

Morning Post.—"Mr. Ernest Vizetelly has given . . . a very true insight into the aims, character, and life of the novelist."

Athenæum.—". . . Exhaustive and interesting."

MEMOIRS OF THE MARTYR KING : being a

detailed record of the last two years of the Reign of His Most Sacred Majesty King Charles the First, 1646–1648–9. Compiled by ALLAN FEA. With upwards of 100 Photogravure Portraits and other Illustrations, including relics. Royal 4to. 105s. net.

Mr. M. H. SPIELMANN in *The Academy.*—"The volume is a triumph for the printer and publisher, and a solid contribution to Carolinian literature"

Pall Mall Gazette.—"The present sumptuous volume, a storehouse of eloquent associations . . comes as near to outward perfection as anything we could desire."

MEMOIRS OF A VANISHED GENERATION

1813–1855. Edited by MRS. WARRENNE BLAKE. With numerous Illustrations. Demy 8vo. 16s. net.

*** *This work is compiled from diaries and letters dating from the time of the Regency to the middle of the nineteenth century. The value of the work lies in its natural unembellished picture of the life of a cultured and well-born family in a foreign environment at a period so close to our own that it is far less familiar than periods much more remote. There is an atmosphere of Jane Austen's novels about the lives of Admiral Knox and his family, and a large number of well-known contemporaries are introduced into Mrs. Blake's pages.*

CÉSAR FRANCK : A Study. Translated from the

French of Vincent d'Indy, with an Introduction by ROSA NEWMARCH. Demy 8vo. 7s. 6d. net.

*** *There is no purer influence in modern music than that of César Franck, for many years ignored in every capacity save that of organist of Sainte-Clotilde, in Paris, but now recognised as the legitimate successor of Bach and Beethoven. His inspiration "rooted in love and faith" has contributed in a remarkable degree to the regeneration of the musical art in France and elsewhere. The now famous "Schola Cantorum," founded in Paris in 1896, by A. Guilmant, Charles Bordes and Vincent d'Indy, is the direct outcome of his influence. Among the artists who were in some sort his disciples were Paul Dukas, Chabrier, Gabriel Fauré and the great violinist Ysaye. His pupils include such gifted composers as Benoît, Augusta Holmès, Chausson, Ropartz, and d'Indy, This book, written with the devotion of a disciple and the authority of a master, leaves us with a vivid and touching impression of the saint-like composer of "The Beatitudes."*

FRENCH NOVELISTS OF TO-DAY : Maurice

Barres, Réné Bazin, Paul Bourget, Pierre de Coulevain, Anatole France, Pierre Loti, Marcel Prévost, and Edouard Rod. Biographical, Descriptive, and Critical. By WINIFRED STEPHENS. With Portraits and Bibliographies. Crown 8vo. 5s. net.

*** *The writer, who has lived much in France, is thoroughly acquainted with French life and with the principal currents of French thought. The book is intended to be a guide to English readers desirous to keep in touch with the best present-day French fiction Special attention is given to the ecclesiastical, social, and intellectual problems of contemporary France and their influence upon the works of French novelists of to-day.*

THE KING'S GENERAL IN THE WEST,

being the Life of Sir Richard Granville, Baronet (1600–1659). By ROGER GRANVILLE, M.A., Sub-Dean of Exeter Cathedral. With Illustrations. Demy 8vo. 10s. 6d. net.

Westminster Gazette.—"A distinctly interesting work; it will be highly appreciated by historical students as well as by ordinary readers."

THE SOUL OF A TURK. By Mrs. DE BUNSEN.
With 8 Full-page Illustrations. Demy 8vo. 10s. 6d. net.

₊ *We hear of Moslem "fanaticism" and Christian "superstition," but it is not easy to find a book which goes to the heart of the matter. "The Soul of a Turk" is the outcome of several journeys in Asiatic and European Turkey, notably one through the Armenian provinces, down the Tigris on a raft to Baghdad and across the Syrian Desert to Damascus Mrs. de Bunsen made a special study of the various forms of religion existing in those countries. Here, side by side with the formal ceremonial of the village mosque and the Christian Church, is the resort to Magic and Mystery.*

THE LIFE AND LETTERS OF ROBERT
STEPHEN HAWKER, sometime Vicar of Morwenstow in Cornwall. By C. E. BYLES. With numerous Illustrations by J. LEY PETHYBRIDGE and others. Demy 8vo. 7s. 6d. net.

Daily Telegraph.—" . . . As soon as the volume is opened one finds oneself in the presence of a real original, a man of ability, genius and eccentricity, of whom one cannot know too much . . . No one will read this fascinating and charmingly produced book without thanks to Mr. Byles and a desire to visit—or revisit—Morwenstow."

THE LIFE OF WILLIAM BLAKE. By ALEXANDER
GILCHRIST. Edited with an Introduction by W. GRAHAM ROBERTSON. Numerous Reproductions from Blake's most characteristic and remarkable designs. Demy 8vo. 10s. 6d. net. New Edition.

Birmingham Post.—"Nothing seems at all likely ever to supplant the Gilchrist biography. Mr. Swinburne praised it magnificently in his own eloquent essay on Blake, and there should be no need now to point out its entire sanity, understanding keenness of critical insight, and masterly literary style. Dealing with one of the most difficult of subjects, it ranks among the finest things of its kind that we possess."

GEORGE MEREDITH : Some Characteristics.
By RICHARD LE GALLIENNE. With a Bibliography (much enlarged) by JOHN LANE. Portrait, etc. Crown 8vo. 5s. net. Fifth Edition. Revised.

Punch.—"All Meredithians must possess 'George Meredith; Some Characteristics,' by Richard Le Gallienne. This book is a complete and excellent guide to the novelist and the novels, a sort of Meredithian Bradshaw, with pictures of the traffic superintendent and the head office at Boxhill. Even *P*hilistines may be won over by the blandishments of Mr Le Gallienne."

LIFE OF LORD CHESTERFIELD. An account
of the Ancestry, Personal Character, and Public Services of the Fourth Earl of Chesterfield. By W. H. CRAIG, M.A. Numerous Illustrations. Demy 8vo. 12s. 6d. net.

Times.—" It is the chief point of Mr. Craig's book to show the sterling qualities which Chesterfield was at too much pains in concealing, to reject the perishable trivialities of his character, and to exhibit him as a philosophic statesman, not inferior to any of his
  f hic life and Chatham at the other."

A QUEEN OF INDISCRETIONS. The Tragedy of Caroline of Brunswick, Queen of England. From the Italian of G. P. CLERICI. Translated by FREDERIC CHAPMAN. With numerous Illustrations reproduced from contemporary Portraits and Prints. Demy 8vo. 21s. net.

The Daily Telegraph.—"It could scarcely be done more thoroughly or, on the whole, in better taste than is here displayed by Professor Clerici. Mr. Frederic Chapman himself contributes an uncommonly interesting and well-informed introduction.'

LETTERS AND JOURNALS OF SAMUEL GRIDLEY HOWE. Edited by his Daughter LAURA E. RICHARDS. With Notes and a Preface by F. B. SANBORN, an Introduction by Mrs. JOHN LANE, and a Portrait. Demy 8vo (9 × 5¾ inches). 16s. net.

Outlook.—"This deeply interesting record of experience. The volume is worthily produced and contains a striking portrait of Howe."

GRIEG AND HIS MUSIC. By H. T. FINCK, Author of "Wagner and his Works," etc. With Illustrations. Crown 8vo. 7s. 6d. net.

EDWARD A. MACDOWELL : a Biography. By LAWRENCE GILMAN, Author of "Phases of Modern Music," "Straus's 'Salome,'" "The Music of To-morrow and Other Studies," "Edward Macdowell," etc. Profusely illustrated. Crown 8vo. 5s. net.

THE LIFE OF ST. MARY MAGDALEN. Translated from the Italian of an Unknown Fourteenth-Century Writer by VALENTINA HAWTREY. With an Introductory Note by VERNON LEE, and 14 Full-page Reproductions from the Old Masters. Crown 8vo. 5s. net.

Daily News —"Miss Valentina Hawtrey has given a most excellent English version of this pleasant work."

MEN AND LETTERS. By HERBERT PAUL, M.P. Fourth Edition. Crown 8vo. 5s. net.

Daily News —"Mr Herbert Paul has done scholars and the reading world in genera a high service in publishing this collection of his essays."

ROBERT BROWNING : Essays and Thoughts. By J. T. NETTLESHIP. With Portrait. Crown 8vo. 5s. 6d. net. Third Edition

WILLIAM MAKEPEACE THACKERAY. A

Biography by Lewis Melville. With 2 Photogravures and numerous other Illustrations. Demy 8vo (9 × 5¾ inches). 25s. net.

₊ *In compiling this biography of Thackeray Mr. Lewis Melville, who is admittedly the authority on the subject, has been assisted by numerous Thackeray experts. Mr. Melville's name has long been associated with Thackeray, not only as founder of the Titmarsh Club, but also as the author of "The Thackeray County" and the editor of the standard edition of Thackeray's works and "Thackeray's Stray Papers." For many years Mr. Melville has devoted himself to the collection of material relating to the life and work of his subject. He has had access to many new letters, and much information has come to hand since the publication of "The Life of Thackeray." Now that everything about the novelist is known, it seems that an appropriate moment has arrived for a new biography. Mr. Melville has also compiled a bibliography of Thackeray that runs to upwards 1,300 items, by many hundreds more than contained in any hitherto issued. This section will be invaluable to the collector. Thackeray's speeches, including several never before republished, have also been collected. There is a list of portraits of the novelist, and a separate index to the Bibliography.*

A LATER PEPYS. The Correspondence of Sir

William Weller Pepys, Bart., Master in Chancery, 1758–1825, with Mrs. Chapone, Mrs. Hartley, Mrs. Montague, Hannah More, William Franks, Sir James Macdonald, Major Rennell, Sir Nathaniel Wraxall, and others. Edited, with an Introduction and Notes, by Alice C. C. Gaussen. With numerous Illustrations. Demy 8vo. In Two Volumes. 32s. net.

Douglas Sladen in the *Queen*.—"This is indisputably a most valuable contribution to the literature of the eighteenth century. It is a veritable storehouse of society gossip, the art criticism, and the mots of famous people."

ROBERT LOUIS STEVENSON, AN ELEGY;

AND OTHER POEMS, MAINLY PERSONAL. By Richard Le Gallienne. Crown 8vo. 4s. 6d. net.

Globe.—"The opening Elegy on R. L. Stevenson includes some tender and touching passages, and has throughout the merits of sincerity and clearness."

RUDYARD KIPLING : a Criticism. By Richard

Le Gallienne. With a Bibliography by John Lane. Crown 8vo. 3s. 6d. net.

Scotsman—"It shows a keen insight into the essential qualities of literature, and analyses Mr Kipling's product with the skill of a craftsman . . . the positive and outstanding merits of Mr. Kipling's contribution to the literature of his time are marshalled by his critic with quite uncommon skill."

APOLOGIA DIFFIDENTIS. By W. Compton

Leith. Demy 8vo. 7s. 6d. net.

₊ *The book, which is largely autobiographical, describes the effect of diffidence upon an individual life, and contains, with a consideration of the nature of shyness, a plea for a kindlier judgment of the inveterate case.*

Daily Mail.—"Mr Leith has written a very beautiful book, and perhaps the publisher's

THE TRUE STORY OF MY LIFE : an Auto-
biography by ALICE M. DIEHL, Novelist, Writer, and Musician.
Demy 8vo. 10s. 6d. net.

THE LIFE OF W. J. FOX, Public Teacher and
Social Reformer, 1786–1864. By the late RICHARD GARNETT,
C.B., LL.D., concluded by EDWARD GARNETT. Demy 8vo.
(9 × 5¾inches.) 16s. net.

₊ *W. J. Fox was a prominent figure in public life from 1820 to 1860. From a weaver's boy he became M.P. for Oldham (1847–1862), and he will always be remembered for his association with South Place Chapel, where his Radical opinions and fame as a preacher and popular orator brought him in contact with an advanced circle of thoughtful people. He was the discoverer of the youthful Robert Browning and Harriet Martineau, and the friend of J. S. Mill, Horne, John Forster, Macready, etc. As an Anti-Corn Law orator, he swayed, by the power of his eloquence, enthusiastic audiences. As a politician, he was the unswerving champion of social reform and the cause of oppressed nationalities, his most celebrated speech being in support of his Bill for National Education, 1850, a Bill which anticipated many of the features of the Education Bill of our own time. He died in 1863. The present Life has been compiled from manuscript material entrusted to Dr. Garnett by Mrs. Bridell Fox.*

OTIA : Essays. By ARMINE THOMAS KENT. Crown
8vo. 5s. net.

TERRORS OF THE LAW : being the Portraits
of Three Lawyers—the original Weir of Hermiston, "Bloody
Jeffreys," and "Bluidy Advocate Mackenzie." By FRANCIS
WATT. With 3 Photogravure Portraits. Fcap. 8vo. 4s. 6d. net.

The Literary World.—"The book is altogether entertaining; it is brisk, lively, and effective. Mr. Watt has already, in his two series of 'The Law's Lumber Room,' established his place as an essayist in legal lore, and the present book will increase his reputation."

CHAMPIONS OF THE FLEET. Captains and
Men-of-War in the Days that Helped to make the Empire. By
EDWARD FRASER. With 16 Full-page Illustrations. Crown 8vo.
6s.

THE LONDONS OF THE BRITISH FLEET :
The Story of Ships bearing the name of Old Renown in Naval
Annals. By EDWARD FRASER. With 8 Illustrations in colours,
and 20 in black and white. Crown 8vo. 6s.

9781333234010

SD - #0106 - 130223 - C0 - 229/152/12 - PB - 9781333234010 - Gloss Lamination